Clarence T

CONFRONTING THE FUTURE

Clarence Thomas

CONFRONTING THE FUTURE

❏

Selections from the Senate Confirmation Hearings and Prior Speeches

❏

INTRODUCTION BY L. GORDON CROVITZ

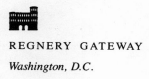

REGNERY GATEWAY

Washington, D.C.

Publisher's Note:
All testimony contained herein was taken directly from the Senate Judiciary Committee's transcripts of the Clarence Thomas Senate Confirmation Hearings. No effort was made to correct punctuation or otherwise alter the testimony.

Library of Congress Cataloging-in-Publication Data
Thomas, Clarence, 1948–
    Clarence Thomas—confronting the future : selections from the
Senate confirmation hearings and prior speeches / introduction by
Gordon Crovitz.
        p.   cm.
    ISBN 0-89526-734-9 (alk. paper)
    1. Thomas, Clarence, 1948–   .   2. United States. Supreme Court.—
Officials and employees—Selection and appointment.   3. Judges—
United States—Selection and appointment.   4. Political questions
and judicial power—United States.   I. United States. Congress.
Senate. Committee on the Judiciary.   II. Title.   III. Title:
Confronting the future.
KF8745.T48A4   1992
347.73'2634—dc20
[347.3073534]   91-46764
                                                       CIP

Published in the United States by
Regnery Gateway
1130 17th Street, NW
Washington, DC 20036

Distributed to the trade by
National Book Network
4720-A Boston Way
Lanham, MD 20706

Cover photograph courtesy of Bettmann Archives

Printed on acid free paper

Manufactured in the United States of America

10 9 8 7 6 5 4 3 2 1

ACKNOWLEDGEMENTS

We wish to thank Deborah Graham Kiley, former director of communications and legislative affairs at the U.S. Equal Employment Opportunity Commission, who so ably and quickly edited the Senate testimony and other materials to make this book. Our most sincere thanks also to Bob Woodson and to R. Gaull Silberman for their advice and counsel regarding the book format and its contents. Most importantly, we want to thank Clarence Thomas for his courage, his convictions, his dignity, and for the example he set for us all.

ACKNOWLEDGMENTS

INTRODUCTION
By L. Gordon Crovitz

In an earlier era, a slave named Dred Scott sued for his freedom, arguing that he was a free man because his owner had taken him to a free state. The Supreme Court ruled against Scott, reminding black Americans that they did not yet possess the full rights of citizenship. A Civil War finally did give blacks the legal guarantee of equality under law. Yet during the summer and fall of 1991, another black man endured a battle that reminded the country that there never was an easy path in the long march to freedom from the plantation.

This time, the nomination of Clarence Thomas to the Supreme Court of the United States unleashed a political force that demanded that all blacks must remain on its ideological plantation. American liberalism, long accustomed to speaking "for blacks," could not bear the prospect of a well-qualified, conservative black achieving the nation's highest judicial office. So the country experienced perhaps the most concentrated and demeaning political attack ever launched against a nominee for high office.

Clarence Thomas is now Justice Clarence Thomas. He survived this process and escaped the liberal plantation. Even more, he prevailed against his critics without lowering himself to their level of destructive politics. At the end of a process that included few other redeeming qualities, he achieved a liberation for all independent-minded people of all races who are willing to pay the price of apostasy from the "politically correct" view.

In a conversation during the hearings, even before Anita Hill made her accusations against him, Justice Thomas described to me an ironic political cartoon he would like to have seen drawn. With his background in segregationist Pin Point, Georgia, the cartoon would start with a group of Ku Klux Klanners hunting down a black man with guns. The cartoon would show him escaping this danger only to turn a corner to be confronted by another mortal enemy. This would be a group of liberal senators and behind-the-scenes aides and lobbyists armed with shotguns, hounds and lynching ropes to stop the black man.

Justice Thomas had no illusions before he was nominated to the Supreme Court that if he ever were nominated it would be an easy process. Less than a month before Justice Thurgood Marshall announced his resignation and President Bush nominated Justice Thomas to succeed him, I had an opportunity to ask him what he thought about his prospects if he were ever nominated. He told me that he would expect his political opponents to try to stop him, that the fight would be rough, but he was philosophical: "I enjoy working here on the federal court of appeals and if I didn't make it, I'd be happy here for the rest of my life." Justice Thomas did not know then how brutal the fight would be—and during the hearings he would say that if he knew at the beginning what would happen to him he would not have accepted the nomination. Still, he was politically sophisticated enough after a decade in office in Washington to know before his nomination that the issue would not be confined to his qualifications for the job. No one could anticipate just how low the battle against him would become.

This book sets out the written record of the final weekend before the vote to confirm Justice Thomas. More than 85% of the American public watched the televised hearing, a figure unmatched even by Super Bowls, World Series and presidential speeches. By overwhelming numbers, people—white and black, male and female—concluded that Judge Thomas deserved to become Justice Thomas. They also concluded that the Senate of the United States had become a partisan gutter of leaks, smears and character assassination.

A woman who had worked for Justice Thomas at the Equal Employment Opportunity Commission was forced by strategic leaking to the press—a media that sacrificed its objectivity at several points during this process—and overwhelming political pressure to testify publicly against him, despite her wishes never to do so. In a sense, University of Oklahoma Law Professor Anita Hill was also a victim of this process. All of this occurred not in the name of the Senate's power to "advise and consent" to presidential nominees to the Supreme Court, but to serve the ends of a minority of partisan senators, their secretive staff members and several special interest groups that could not condone a black conservative justice.

One reason Justice Thomas drew the venom of the liberal special interest groups is that he was at the center of an intellectual debate led by blacks who by the mid-1980s began to doubt the wisdom of some of the more extreme affirmative-action programs. These plans were designed with the best of intentions to bring minorities into our colleges, professions and businesses. Many blacks, including Justice Thomas, publicly worried that this road built of good intentions now leads a generation of minorities down a dangerous path.

Thomas Sowell of the Hoover Institution, one of the nation's leading economists, has published widely on the unintended effects of affirmative action. His worldwide survey, "Preferential Policies: An International Perspective," found that affirmative-action programs tend to benefit only more affluent members of the targeted minority group, leaving the less fortunate members of the group to suffer the cultural backlash from those who resent preferential programs for others.

Even black scholars who are not conservatives now make similar arguments. The Thomas nomination "touches the very soul of the debate in black America, which is a debate between using the principle of self-sufficiency as a means of power as opposed to using our history of victimization," Shelby Steele, author of "The Content of Our Character," said. He added,

"Watch out that your closest friend may be your greatest enemy, is my feeling about liberals, because they encourage us to identify with our victimization. . . . This is racial exploitation by white liberals, who transform this into their own source of power. We're being had by them, and we really need to know that."

Yale Law Professor Stephen Carter has written about the two-edged sword of affirmative action. In "Reflections of an Affirmative Action Baby," published a few months before the Thomas hearings, Mr. Carter criticized affirmative action for furthering the racist stereotype that blacks can aspire only to being the best black, not the best. He also made the point that blacks who belong to the so-called underclass of mostly urban poor do not benefit from these programs, which deflect attention away from the critical problems of a failed public school system and a criminal-justice system that in many neighborhoods no longer protects law-abiding citizens.

Indeed, this nomination was about much more than a seat on the Supreme Court. "Judge Thomas, by virtue of both life experience and philosophy, has become a metaphor for self-reliance and self-development," Robert Woodson, president of the National Center for Neighborhood Enterprise, said. "Traditional race-based proposals such as affirmative action are now being challenged by those who promote self-reliant initiatives." Mr. Woodson noted that opinion polls found that lower-income blacks overwhelmingly supported the nomination, while the wealthiest blacks tended to oppose it.

This split reflects a long-time division within the black community, which has been exacerbated by the continuing problems of a poor underclass. Booker T. Washington, founder of Tuskegee Institute, also founded the National Negro Business League in 1900 to promote economic independence. "Negroes should create their own opportunities," he said. "What a mighty power we shall be when we begin this, and we shall never be a mighty power until we do begin." The NAACP at the time vilified Washington, distorting his views in much the same way that some tried to caricature Justice Thomas's views as being insensitive to the racism that surely does continue.

Marcus Garvey followed in the Washington tradition. He too was bitterly denounced by the civil rights groups. Even S. B. Fuller, who early this century built a fortune from a modest beginning in door-to-door sales, was rewarded with a call for a boycott by the civil rights groups when he gave a speech in 1963 urging a stronger embrace by blacks of the "capitalist system" as the best hope out of poverty.

During Justice Thomas's first set of confirmation hearings, before the Anita Hill accusations, Senator Joseph Biden questioned him closely on the issue of economic liberties under the Constitution. These rights, which protect private property and freedom of contract, fell out of judicial favor during the New Deal when government began intervening deeply into markets. Indeed, Senator Biden began the hearings not by asking about affirmative action or abortion, but about constitutional rights for property. Senator Biden was skeptical about the importance of these rights, and asked Justice Thomas why he had given speeches asserting that under the Constitution, "Economic rights are protected as much as any other rights."

Justice Thomas told the senators that it was the failure of courts that made Jim Crow segregation possible. Judges failed to protect the property rights of blacks during this era to work and enjoy the fruits of their labor. He recalled that his grandfather was always at risk of losing his license to drive the oil-delivery truck; arbitrarily denying blacks licenses—effectively robbing them of the right to earn—was a devastatingly effective method of discrimination.

In 1985, Justice Thomas gave one of the most eloquent speeches ever delivered on the challenges facing black Americans. Very much in the Washington-Garvey-Fuller tradition of self-help with an emphasis on economic advancement, Justice Thomas's theme in his commencement speech at Savannah State

College, which is printed in this volume, was that blacks must rely on more than the great civil rights victories of the 1960s. Justice Thomas invited the strong opposition of liberal groups, including many of the established civil rights organizations, for daring to assert that their agenda and the hegemony of their ideology in many ways left blacks worse off than they were before.

"I had the benefit of people who knew they had to walk a straighter line, climb a taller mountain, and carry a heavier load," Justice Thomas told the graduates. "You all have a much tougher road to travel. Not only do you have to contend with the ever-present bigotry, you must do so with a recent tradition that almost requires you to wallow in excuses. You now have a popular national rhetoric which says that you can't learn because of racism, you can't raise the babies you make because of racism, you can't get up in the mornings because of racism. You commit crimes because of racism. Unlike me you must not only overcome the repressiveness of racism, you must also overcome the lure of excuses. You have twice the job I had."

He concluded his commencement speech with comments that proved prophetic in his own case. He described two roads, one where "a race of people is rushing mindlessly down a highway of sweet, intoxicating destruction, with all its bright lights and grand promises, constructed by social scientists and politicians." The other road, the one he said was less travelled by, is the "road that *might* reward hard work and discipline; that *might* reward intelligence; that *might* be fair and provide equal opportunity. But there are no guarantees."

Justice Thomas was reminded that there are no guarantees soon after his nomination when the smears began. His qualifications for the job were impressive, despite his young age of 43. He overcame the segregation of his youth in Georgia, did well at Yale Law School and worked as a lawyer in every branch of government. He worked in the executive branch first as an assistant attorney general in Missouri, then later at the U.S.

Education Department and as chairman of the Equal Employment Opportunity Commission. He worked on the legislative
staff of Senator John Danforth, Republican of Missouri. For
more than a year before his nomination, he served as a federal
appeals court judge on the District of Columbia Circuit, which
hears many of the country's most significant legal cases.

Unlike many nominees, including his immediate predecessor
as a nominee, David Souter, Justice Thomas was familiar with
many of the federal legal issues that come before the Supreme
Court, from agency-lawmaking questions to separation of
powers to criminal procedural rights. President Bush called
Justice Thomas the best-qualified person for the job. Those who
noted that Robert Bork had an even more impressive paper
record would later acknowledge that Justice Thomas, learning
from the attacks on nominee Bork, was more successful in
deflecting the political smears.

Throughout the summer, opinion polls found that an overwhelming percentage of Americans favored the nomination. A
Gallup Poll found that 57% of blacks favored Justice Thomas,
with only 18% opposing. Black civil rights groups were split.
The national board of the NAACP, which was particularly
heavily lobbied by its labor-union members, chose to oppose the
nomination. Margaret Bush Wilson, who was the NAACP national board chairwoman for a decade until 1984, publicly
supported Justice Thomas. So, too, did several local chapters of
the NAACP. The Compton, California, branch endured threats
of expulsion to endorse Justice Thomas.

None of Justice Thomas's accomplishments could spare him
the smears that by 1991 were the leading weapon of liberals
against conservative nominees whose views were shared by
most Americans. "We're going to Bork him," Florence Kennedy
declared, signalling the strategy of the liberal National Organization for Women. "We're going to kill him politically," she
promised, asking, "This little creep, where did he come from?"
Some liberal blacks were no less tolerant of this conservative

nominee. Derrick Bell, a Harvard law professor, said that Justice Thomas "doesn't think like a black." Columnist Carl Rowan declared that "If you give Clarence Thomas a little flour on his face, you'd think you had David Duke."

The Borking began in earnest within days of the nomination. He was accused of being an anti-Semite for his comments in 1983 praising Louis Farrahkan; Justice Thomas did approve Mr. Farrahkan's self-help message for blacks, but disassociated himself with the messenger when Mr. Farrahkan made comments disparaging Jews. In 1986, the Orthodox Jewish Congregations of America awarded Justice Thomas with its annual Humanitarian Award for his work at the EEOC. Justice Thomas was also accused of being too Catholic, with Virginia Governor Douglas Wilder asking, "How much allegiance does [Justice Thomas] have to the Pope?" Whatever the appropriateness of such a remark, it soon became known that Justice Thomas attends an Episcopalian church. Reporters sneaked into his garage to rummage through some of his books, but they found nothing more prurient than works by Alexander Solzhenitsyn and Ayn Rand. He was accused of displaying a Confederate flag in his office in the Missouri attorney general's office, but it turned out this flag was the state flag of his home, Georgia.

People for the American Way, the group associated with television producer Norman Lear, issued press releases saying that Justice Thomas had violated EEOC travel rules when he spoke to several law schools. There was no suggestion that Justice Thomas ever abused his travels for personal gain, but the lobbying group claimed that these speeches went beyond the official business of the EEOC chairman. This was quickly dismissed when a review of past records showed that speaking to law schools has been an important part of the job.

The Senate Judiciary Committee, whose liberal members and staff led the battle against the Bork nomination exactly four years earlier, set out to scan Justice Thomas's written record for anything that could be twisted for use against him. There was a "document request" asking for nearly everything Justice Thomas had ever said, written or approved. Justice Thomas provided the committee with 32,000 documents. The only precedent was a similarly huge request for documents that the Senate committee used to block the nomination of another conservative black, William Lucas, who President Bush had nominated to be the assistant attorney general in charge of the civil rights division.

None of these mudballs stuck to Justice Thomas. On September 27, the Senate Judiciary Committee voted in a partisan 7-7 split to recommend his nomination to the full Senate. Senators voted knowing about Ms. Hill's accusations, but had judged them too far-fetched to warrant further consideration. This was especially so because she insisted on anonymity. It appeared that Justice Thomas would soon be confirmed by a comfortable margin in the full Senate. But then he was tackled on the threshold of the entry to the Supreme Court.

As the hours approached for the final vote, liberal special interest groups busily made blind phone calls to people who had worked with Justice Thomas, seeking any information that could be used against him. Even Senator Howard Metzenbaum admitted on the Senate floor that his staff had made many calls looking for anything they could find to help to defeat the nomination. Past workers at the EEOC complained that they received numerous phone calls asking for any kind of dirt on Justice Thomas. Perhaps hundreds or even thousands of such calls were made. It was not surprising that one person eventually did come forward—even if it was not by her own wishes.

On September 25, when agents from the Federal Bureau of Investigation informed him that there had been a serious accusation against him by a woman who had worked with him, the full significance of the opposition to Justice Thomas became clear. "When informed by the FBI agents of the nature of the allegations and the person making them, I was shocked, surprised, hurt and enormously saddened," Justice Thomas told the Senate Judiciary Committee when they reconvened their hearings specifically to inquire into the charges. "I have been racking my brains and eating my insides out trying to think of what I could have said or done to Anita Hill to lead her to allege that I was interested in her in more than a professional way."

Behind the scenes, however, the Anita Hill-Clarence Thomas confrontation had been planned for weeks, perhaps months. The full chronology of how Ms. Hill's accusations became public and led to the gripping hearings is important for seeing how politics and scandals operate today in Washington:

On July 1, President Bush nominated Clarence Thomas to the Supreme Court.

On July 28, an article in the Boston Globe reported: "The major civil rights and civil liberties organizations, many of them led by veterans of the Bork battles, are sharing research and coordinating strategy. . . . The official said, for instance, that opposition groups have been withholding some damaging information about Thomas's record, and will time its release to achieve maximum impact."

In early September, a Labor Committee aide to Senator Edward Kennedy, Ricki Seidman, contacted Ms. Hill, who didn't lodge her accusation in that conversation. Ms. Seidman had joined the Senate staff in July 1991, *after* Clarence Thomas was nominated; she previously had served as chief investigator for People for the American Way and also was well known in Washington for her role in defeating Robert Bork.

On September 9, Ms. Hill said she was willing to talk about her complaint. Ms. Seidman referred her to another Labor Committee aide, James Brudney, who works for Senator Howard Metzenbaum and attended Yale Law School with Ms. Hill. The next day, Mr. Brudney gave the allegations to Harriet Grant, the Judiciary Committee's chief nomination counsel. Ms. Hill called the Judiciary Committee for the first time on September 12. Senator Biden later said that Ms. Hill wanted her allegation kept "completely confidential."

On September 18, a friend of Ms. Hill called the committee to offer some corroborating support. On September 19, Ms. Hill called to say that she wanted all of the committee's members to know about her complaint, and lifted her anonymity request. It was during this period that Ms. Hill consulted law school friends and civil rights activists.

On September 23, Ms. Hill agreed to have her name used when the FBI interviewed Justice Thomas about her charges. The FBI report was completed on September 25 and that evening Senators Biden and Thurmond told the rest of the panel about the allegations. Senator Biden briefed each Democrat orally and brought along copies of the FBI report and of Ms. Hill's statement, if any wished to read it. On Friday, September 27, Mr. Biden gave all relevant documents to all of the committee Democrats. The committee then voted to send the nomination to the full Senate for a scheduled October 8 vote.

On October 4, Friday, Senator Orrin Hatch predicted an attempt would be made over the weekend to stop the nomination. It was indeed over this weekend that someone "outed" Ms. Hill and her charges against Judge Thomas by leaking her Judiciary Committee statement. On Sunday morning, October 6, the Hill allegation appeared in *Newsday* and in a report by Nina Totenberg on Public Radio's "Weekend Edition." Interviewed on the program, Ms. Totenberg said: "I heard about it from a number of sources. I did reach her. She refused to talk to me at all until I had obtained a copy of her affidavit. She then confirmed its authenticity and agreed to talk."

Ms. Hill testified that she never intended her charges to be made public, but felt obliged to testify once the leak occurred. Indeed, she also testified that James Brudney, Senator Metzenbaum's aide, told her that Justice Thomas might quietly withdraw his nomination once he heard about her charges. In other words, she was being told that she might be able to stop the nomination without ever having to go public.

Even before the second set of hearings began, many people

wondered about Ms. Hill's charge that Justice Thomas had made unwanted advances and mentioned pornographic material to her. She had followed him from the Education Department to the EEOC despite the alleged harassment and had stayed in touch with him over the years. It turned out that there was a telephone log of calls into Justice Thomas's office when he was at the EEOC. The log included 11 calls to Justice Thomas from Ms. Hill between 1984 and 1990. It reads as follows:

January 31, 1984, 11:50 A.M. "Just called to say hello. Sorry she didn't get to see you last week."

May 9, 1984, 11:40 A.M. "Pls call."

August 29, 1984, 4:59 P.M. "Needs your advice on getting research grants."

August 30, 1984, 11:55 A.M. "Returned your call (call btwn 1 & 4)."

January 3, 1985, 3:40 P.M. "Pls call tonight." On this message Ms. Hill leaves the phone number for the Embassy Row Hotel in Washington and a room number.

February 26, 1985, 5:50 P.M. "Pls call."

March 4, 1985, 11:15 A.M. "Pls call re: research project."

March 4, 1985, 11:25 A.M. Call from Susan Cahall "w/ Tulsa EEO ofc. Referred by Anita to see if you would come to Tulsa on 3/27 to speak at an EEO conference."

July 5, 1985, 1:30 P.M. "Pls call."

October 8, 1986, 12:25 P.M. "Pls call."

August 4, 1987, 4 P.M. "In town 'til 8/15 . . . wanted to congratulate on marriage."

November 1, 1990, 11:40 A.M. "Re speaking engagement at University of Oklahoma School of Law."

At first, Ms. Hill called the logs "garbage," but later admitted the calls were made. Her defenders argued that it is not uncommon for victims of harassment to remain quiet for many years.

Readers can follow the charges, defenses and countercharges as they were made in the hearings. The transcript selections reprinted here will make fascinating reading for as many years as we have public spectacles where nominees to high public office must, if they become controversial enough, defend themselves from the most scurrilous attacks.

Where did Justice Thomas find the strength to persevere? He was shocked all the more by the charges because they were made by someone he thought he knew, and for whom he had served as a mentor. He had tried to help Ms. Hill's career, despite their political differences. He wrote a letter of recommendation for her to join the faculty of Oral Roberts Law School that included the political caveat that "we have disagreed on the positions to be taken in particular matters." Phyllis Berry-Myers, who worked closely with both Justice Thomas and Ms. Hill at the EEOC, said that Ms. Hill "was not a Reagan Republican" and was "a lot more liberal in her thinking than Justice Thomas." Still, Justice Thomas was surprised to hear that Ms. Hill opposed his nomination.

Virginia Lamp Thomas, his wife, gave an important explanation for the source of Justice Thomas's resolve to fight back in an article she wrote about the nomination in *People* magazine. She disclosed the importance of their religious faith in confronting the accusations. Mrs. Thomas, who wrote that, "In my heart I always believed [Anita Hill] was probably in love with my husband and never got what she wanted," recalled that Justice Thomas asked her to organize prayer sessions on the eve of the hearing.

"The Clarence Thomas I had married was nowhere to be found. He was just debilitated beyond anything I had seen in my life," she wrote. "He said, 'I need you to call your two friends from your Bible-study group, and their husbands, and get them with me in the morning to pray.' Clarence knew the next round of hearings to begin that day was not the normal political battle. It was spiritual warfare. Good versus evil. We were fighting something we didn't understand, and we needed prayerful people in our lives. We needed God."

It was significant that the first point Justice Thomas made in his opening statement was that only his wife and Senator Danforth had heard the statement, "no handlers, no advisers." In her *People* magazine article, Mrs. Thomas described how he prepared the statement:

"All the strategists were pushed out the door—all the handlers, these people telling Clarence what he should do and say at the next morning's hearing. He started getting real tense in the neck. He hadn't slept the last two nights. Then about 9 P.M., we got word that Clarence would be the first to talk at the hearing. I called a neighbor lady who cuts hair to come over, because Clarence hadn't had a haircut in three months. She cut his hair, gave him a head massage, and he fell asleep around 10:30.

"Around 1 A.M. he woke up, went downstairs and started working. He saw all those papers with his notes about how to respond on the kitchen table and started to get really confused. I tried to be the calming influence, and I cleared the table. Then I went upstairs to turn on the computer, and by the time I came down, he was real focused. He wrote on a pad of paper, and I would type it. We worked like that until 4:30 A.M."

Justice Thomas hoped to salvage his good name and reputation. In the process, he also saved his nomination. He began by telling the Senators, in essence, that they could deny him the Supreme Court position, but he was not going to let them leave him branded a sexual harasser or a fan of pornography. He denied all the charges with a vehemence that seemed to leave many senators speechless, including several who must have hoped he would simply withdraw his name from consideration rather than endure the embarrassment of having to speak in public about the accusations.

His statement gripped the nation because it so clearly came from the heart. Justice Thomas was angry, and he let it show. In a city of hidden agendas, camouflaged ideology and shifting alliances, here finally was a man who had a simple, personal story to tell, and he told it. During the hearings he flatly denied the allegations and suggested that they had been concocted bv the special interest groups with Ms. Hill playing a secondary role. He did not target his anger at Ms. Hill, but instead reserved his greatest anger for the Senators who would decide his fate.

"This is a circus," he told the ringleaders of the Judiciary Committee. "It is a national disgrace. And from my standpoint, as a black American, as far as I am concerned, it is a high-tech lynching for uppity blacks who in any way deign to think for themselves, to do for themselves, to have different ideas, and it is a message that, unless you kow-tow to an old order, this is what will happen to you: You will be lynched, destroyed, caricatured by a committee of the U.S. Senate, rather than hung from a tree."

By the end of the second hearing, opinion polls found that Americans believed Justice Thomas by a margin of more than two to one, with men, women, whites and blacks in close agreement. The view was almost unanimous that the Senate had demeaned the process to an almost unimaginable degree. The same body that sponsored the Joe McCarthy hearings and the self-destructive Iran-Contra affair hearings somehow managed to sink to a new low. Were this hearing reviewed by the board that rates movies, it would clearly deserve an X rating. Here is how an editorial in *The Wall Street Journal* summed up the Hill-Thomas hearing:

"For no matter what one thinks of Anita Hill's allegations against Justice Thomas, the overwhelming impression is that the circus has left every American belittled. Someone must explain how America's public square became a charnel house. Joe Biden blames one 'unfortunate' leak to the media, but that one leak needs to be understood as part of a pattern. The Senate had already wallowed in the pillorying of Robert Bork, in the sexual charges against John Tower. . . . Why should we be surprised that it would take the next step, sinking into the primordial ooze of Long Dong Silver?"

A page-one article in *The Washington Post* reached similar conclusions. "In recent years the confirmation of Supreme

Court nominees has evolved into a Washington melodrama in which private interest groups, journalists and lobbyists have become central players. Assuming a role once played almost exclusively by the Senate, these actors have become de facto adjuncts to the Senate Judiciary Committee, scrutinizing the public and private lives in an effort to defeat nominees they oppose," the *Post* reported with remarkable candor.

"That turn illustrates the increasingly symbiotic relationship between committee staffers, liberal interest groups and the news media. It is a phenomena [sic] that accelerated with the Reagan administration's attempts to ensure conservative domination of the judiciary in the 1980s. Many thought it reached its ultimate expression in the battle over the nomination of Robert H. Bork to the Supreme Court in 1987. But within days after President Bush announced Thomas's nomination, liberal activist groups began the search for ammunition they hoped could defeat him."

Jet magazine, a widely circulated black publication, had its own summary of what had happened. "No black had been so brutalized in American politics," it reported. "Throughout the political ordeal, the old time religion had held together the black family, a small black Republican lobby and white conservative supporters."

Justice Thomas's victory was more than for himself. There are many blacks and other minorities who were once expected to hold only certain political beliefs, but who now can see that the price of apostasy need not be fatal. However, there surely can be a high price to pay. As President Bush said, "The piranha tactics of smearing the individual and ignoring the issue serves no public purpose. They aim to destroy lives and wreck reputations." Justice Thomas will now have a lifetime on the highest court in the land to remind his political enemies why it was that they were willing to go to such lengths to block this nominee. Justice Thomas's energy and intelligence do, indeed, make him a serious threat to the status quo that liberals had hoped to protect.

Justice Thomas is hardly alone among Americans in his resolve to escape the ideological plantation. He saw the political lynching coming, but was unusually well prepared to prevail. His strength of character, firm beliefs and the support of family and faith gave him the freedom to defend himself from partisan attacks.

Freedom of thought, like all forms of liberty, will remain a strong attraction, whatever the risks. At this moment in the history of the United States, this will mean more blacks and other minorities will deign, as Justice Thomas put it, "to think for themselves, to do for themselves, to have different ideas." The determination of Justice Thomas will mean that others will not have to pay the price exacted from him when they follow his example by daring to act on their own personal declarations of independence.

(L. GORDON CROVITZ is assistant editorial page editor of *The Wall Street Journal,* which publishes his weekly "Rule of Law" column. He is a graduate of Yale Law School.)

Clarence Thomas

CONFRONTING THE FUTURE

❏

Senator [ORRIN G.] HATCH. . . . Now, did you ever say to Professor Hill in words or substance, and this is embarrassing for me to say in public, but it has to be done, and I am sure it is not pleasing to you.

Did you ever say in words or substance something like there is a pubic hair in my coke?

Judge THOMAS. No, Senator.

Senator HATCH. Did you ever refer to your private parts in conversations with Professor Hill?

Judge THOMAS. Absolutely not, Senator.

Senator HATCH. Did you ever brag to Professor Hill about your sexual prowess?

Judge THOMAS. No, Senator.

Senator HATCH. Did you ever use the term "Long Dong Silver" in conversation with Professor Hill?

Judge THOMAS. No, Senator.

Senator HATCH. Did you ever have lunch with Professor Hill at which you talked about sex or pressured her to go out with you?

Judge THOMAS. Absolutely not.

Senator HATCH. Did you ever tell—

Judge THOMAS [continuing]. I have had no such discussions, nor have I ever pressured or asked her to go out with me beyond her work environment.

Senator HATCH. Did you ever tell Professor Hill that she should see pornographic films?

Judge THOMAS. Absolutely not.

28 · CLARENCE THOMAS

Senator HATCH. Did you ever talk about pornography with Professor Hill?

Judge THOMAS. I did not discuss any pornographic material or pornographic preferences or pornographic films with Professor Hill.

❑

T hus, *in one of the most poignant exchanges of the extraordinary hearings, Justice Thomas responded to Senator Hatch's recital of charges by accuser Anita F. Hill while Virginia Lamp Thomas sat behind her husband, eyes brimming. Under the glare of television lights, the Senate tribunal interrogated Clarence Thomas—seemingly without regard for his distinguished record of enforcing the law against sexual harassment, his devotion to family and, as witness Carlton Stewart reminded the Judiciary Committee, ". . . separate and apart from Supreme Court confirmation, Clarence Thomas is a sitting Federal Judge." In one incredible weekend, the confirmation of this American called to public service had become a nationwide seminar on our federal legislative process run amok.*

❏

PRESIDENT GEORGE BUSH SAID IN A SPEECH TO PUBLIC ADMINISTRATION GROUPS ON OCT. 24, 1991 IN WASHINGTON, D.C.:

"The recent hearings on Judge Thomas stirred a kind of anger. The American people saw some of the seamier sides of Washington life. They saw proceedings that degenerated into target practice against good men and women. Ronnie Perry of Brunswick, Georgia, wrote me a letter—I don't know him. Here's what it said: "It is my fear that good, honest, moral men and women in this country will no longer subject themselves to the ridicule that Judge Thomas had to face." Likewise, Anita Hill's backers might wonder how anyone might be expected to come forward in the future if public officials cannot maintain proper confidentiality—such as the confidentiality promised to Professor Hill. . . .

"The bruising hearings showed what happens when political factions let agendas overwhelm personal decency. Some people have tried to drag public debate to a new low, searching openly for dirt—any dirt—without regard to people's rights to privacy, sometimes without concern for the facts. While crusading pressure groups talk about their favorite issues, they forget that human beings sit there beneath the glare of the spotlight, vulnerable to assault from all quarters. The piranha tactics of smearing the individual and ignoring the issue serve no public purpose. They aim to destroy lives and wreck reputations.

"The dramatic hearings and the theatrics outside the hearing rooms captivated the attention of the American public, all right. Millions upon millions of Americans watched the hearings with a combination of curiosity, suspense, and I submit to you all, disgust. The nation was stunned and repulsed by the spectacle. The scenes from the Senate bore little resemblance to the tidy legislative process that we all studied in school and that we describe to our children—now, maybe to our grandchildren. X-rated statements, cross-examinations pushed aside the soaps and Saturday cartoons. And the process seemed unreal—more like a satire than like the government in which all of you, in which I, take so much pride; more like a burlesque show than a civics class.

"The hearings also showed that politicians must contend with a host of different forces and influences. The public saw the congressional staffers everywhere; saw outside pressure groups exhorting and twisting—and the staffs ever-present, everywhere.

"I worry that the hearings sent our people this kind of false message: If you want to make a difference, don't enter public service. Join a special interest group. That way, whether it's the right or the left, join a special interest group, and that way you can fight as hard as you want, or as dirty as you want, without any responsibility for the results."

◻

No *single document more eloquently illustrates Clarence Thomas' philosophy of hard work, education, faith and family than his 1985 commencement speech at Savannah State College. Inherent in his message was a challenge to politicians and social activists to make room for new ideas to solve old problems. That oft-repeated challenge made Justice Thomas a threat to the special interests that have dictated for so many years the stagnant social policies of this nation.*

❑

SAVANNAH STATE COLLEGE COMMENCEMENT ADDRESS
BY CLARENCE THOMAS

SAVANNAH, GEORGIA, JUNE 9, 1985

President Rayburn, members of the faculty, distinguished guests, relatives, friends, and most importantly, graduates. It is with great pleasure and a sense of gratitude that I stand before you all today. I regret only that my grandparents, Myers and Christine Anderson, are not here. Not too many years ago, attending Savannah State was a distant dream for me. This institution, the bricks, the mortar, the books, the professors stood as a testament to a race in the defiance of a *system* designed to keep a race ignorant—a *system* bent on establishing racial dominance. Savannah State College, its legacy, its tradition, its history made it possible for those of us who grew up in its benevolent shadows to believe that we could take another giant step away from slavery, that we could leap across the great chasm of bigotry and hatred, that we could one day have what the *other* America had, endless opportunities in a bountiful country. *Yes*, I grew up here in Savannah. *Yes*, I was born not far from here (in Pinpoint) [sic]. I am a child of those marshes, a son of this soil. I am a descendant of the slaves whose labors made the dark soil of the South productive. I am the great, great grandson of a freed slave, whose enslavement continued after my birth. I am, my friends, the product of hatred and love—the hatred of the social and political structure which dominated the segregated, hate-filled city of my youth *and* the love of some people—my mother, my grandparents, my neighbors and relatives—who said *by* their actions "You can make it, but first, you must endure." You *can survive*, but first, you must endure. You *can live*, but first, you must endure. You must endure the unfairness—you must endure the hatred—you must endure the bigotry—you must endure the segregation. You must endure the indignities.

I watched the strongest man in the world endure *so* that he could raise his two grandsons, *so* that he could make something of his life; and *so* that his two grandsons (my brother and me) could do the same with ours. I watched a quiet strong grandmother slave away in the kitchen, clean house, cook *and endure*, so we could make it. I watched through a child's eyes as my young mother, Miss Mariah, Miss Bec, Miss Gladys, Miss Gertrude, Cousin Hattie, Cousin Bea, Cousin Julie all worked countless hours in other people's kitchens, with aching feet and pain-filled heads for little pay and no benefits—but they *endured* so that we who watched them could make it.

They loved us not only with kisses and hugs but with example. I have watched these women line up in the early morning—in the cold—in the dark—in the rain to catch the bus to work. I have watched them in the evenings standing on solitary corners with their shopping bags in the heat and humidity waiting for the bus where they would crowd in the back, with no air-conditioning—or if they were lucky, they would ride in the back seat of their employer's car. They endured *this* to get home dead tired so they could raise *their* families, clean their houses, cook their dinners. And we, we had the nerve to wonder why they needed a goodie, a standback or a BC with a coke. But *endure* they did—and through the eyes of children, we watched.

I haven't mentioned those women who shucked oysters, picked crabs, headed shrimp, hoed corn, raised chickens. I haven't mentioned those men who held two or even three jobs. I haven't mentioned Mr. Miller (both father and son) who worked *all* the time. I haven't mentioned Mr. Sam Williams and Mr. Ben Wise who ran businesses and carried fuel oil like my grandfather. I haven't mentioned all those people who could fix anything or build anything. They endured Savannah and all it had to offer.

I watched through the eyes of a child as my race took that part of life that was left and survived. I often think about the renewed interest in soul food. Take, for example, what we ate from the pig; the foot, the tail, the head, the ears, the neck, and intestines. I have yet to mention any part that anyone else wanted. If someone was having pork shoulder or ham for dinner, we would say "Yeah, they're eating high on the hog." To this day I marvel at what my mother could do with some neckbones and pigtails—and what my grandmother could do with chicken feet.

These are my greatest teachers. My role models. Their lives have been my greatest and most important classes. They made every effort to rise above the life they were left to wallow in. Even though they had to live in poverty or near poverty, they rejected squalor and self-pity. They refused to give in to the seemingly hopeless circumstances, *and* they never gave up. They rose up like a phoenix from the ashes of bigotry and hatred. They endured—they survived. And, we were the beneficiaries of their survival, for we had no choice but to learn the values which made their survival possible *and* the hostility and bigotry which we could expect as we grew older and took our turn at being adults. I learned from people whose condition and status were self-evident but who *refused* to accept as inevitable the rational consequences of their lot.

Today I stand before you as one who had the same beginnings as yourselves—as one who has walked a little farther down the road, climbed a little higher up the mountain. I come back to you, who must now travel this road and climb this jagged, steep mountain that lies ahead. I return as a messenger—a front-runner, a scout. My friends, what lies ahead of you is even tougher than what is now behind you.

That mean, callous world out there is still very much filled with discrimination. It still holds out a different life for those who do not happen to be the right race or the right sex. It is a world in which the "haves" continue to reap more dividends than the "have-nots", and the powerful wield more influence than the powerless.

You will enter a world in which more than one-half of all Black children are born primarily to youthful mothers and out of wedlock. You will enter a world in which the Black teenage unemployment rate as always is more than double that of white teenagers. Yours will be a world in which computers and computer technology are a way of life. Any discrimination, like sharp turns in a road, become [sic] critical because of the tremendous speed at which we are travelling toward and into the high-tech world of a service economy.

Because I was once as youthful as you all are, I am familiar with the omniscience of youthful arrogance. Mr. "Know-t-All" [sic] is what my grandfather called me when he grew weary of me. Accepting this tendency as a given, I urge you to listen anyway.

There is a tendency among young upwardly mobile, intelligent minorities today to forget. We *forget* the sweat of our forefathers. We *forget* the blood of the marchers, the prayers and hope of our race. We *forget* who brought us into this world. We *overlook* who put food in our mouths and clothes on our backs. We forget commitment to excellence. We *procreate* with pleasure and retreat from the responsibilities of the babies we produce. We subdue, we seduce, but we don't respect ourselves, our women, our babies. How do we expect a race that has been thrown into the gutter of socio-economic indicators to rise above these humiliating circumstances if we hide from responsibility for our own destiny. The truth of the matter is we have become more interested in designer jeans and break-dancing than we are in obligations and responsibilities.

Over the past 15 years, I have watched as others have jumped quickly at the opportunity to make excuses for Black Americans. It is said that Blacks cannot start businesses because of discrimination. But, I remember businesses on East Broad and West Broad that were run in spite of bigotry. It is said that we can't learn because of bigotry. But I know for a fact that tens of thousands of Blacks were educated at histori-cally Black colleges, in spite of discrimination. And there are some who would have closed this College in the name of desegregation when they opened up the competitive school as a junior college to keep from going to Savannah State. We learned to read in spite of segregated libraries. You didn't dare go to the Savannah Public Library—Carnegie is where you went. We built homes in spite of segregated neighborhoods. We learned how to play basketball (and did we ever learn!!), even though we couldn't go to the NBA. And you had better not go into Daffin Park.

You ask what am I saying. Simply put, I am saying that we have lost something. We look for role models in all the wrong places. We refuse to reach back in our not too distant past for the lessons and values we need to carry us into the uncertain future. We prefer the speculations of seers and clairvoyants to the certainty of past experience. We ignore what has permitted Blacks in this country to survive the brutality of slavery and the bitter rejection of segregation. We overlook the reality of positive values and run to the mirage of promises, visions and dreams.

I do not stand before you poised for debate. I do not dare come to this city, which only two decades ago clung so

tenaciously to segregation, bigotry, and Jim Crowism, to convince you all of the fairness of this society. My memory is too
precise—my recollection too keen to venture down that path of
self-delusion. I am not blind to our history—nor do I turn a deaf
ear to the pleas and cries of Black Americans. Often I must
struggle to contain my outrage at what has happened to Black
Americans—what continues to happen—what we let happen
and what we do to ourselves. If I let myself go, I would rage in
the words of Frederick Douglass:

> "At a time like this, scorching irony, not convincing
> argument, is needed. Oh! Had I the ability, and could
> reach the nation's ear, I would today pour out a fiery stream
> of biting ridicule, blasting reproach, withering sarcasm
> and stern rebuke. For it is not light that is needed, but fire;
> it is not the gentle shower, but thunder. We need the storm,
> the whirlwind, and the earthquake. The feeling of the
> nation must be quickened; the conscience of the nation
> must be roused; the propriety of the nation must be started;
> the hypocrisy of the nation must be exposed; and its
> crimes against God and man must be denounced."

I often hear rosy platitudes about this country—much of
which is true. It is the greatest country on earth—it does have
more freedoms than any other nation. It is the richest and the
most powerful country. All of this is true, and makes me proud,
but how are we Black Americans to feel when we have so little
in a land with so much. How is Black America to respond to the
celebration of the wonders of this great nation. Again, in the
words of Frederick Douglass:

> "To him, your celebration is a sham; your boasted lib-
> erty, an unholy license; your national greatness, swelling
> vanity; your sounds of rejoicing are empty and heartless;
> your denunciation of tyrants, *brass-fronted* impudence;

your shouts of liberty and equality, hollow mockery; your prayers and hymns, your sermons and thanksgivings, with all your religious parade and solemnity, are to Him mere bombast, fraud, deception, impiety, and hypocrisy. . . ."

No, I have no delusions about discrimination, racism, or bigotry. I am not among those who believed that this unholy triumvirate went some place—disappeared. I watched, however, as those three demons were summoned up or sent away to suit the whims and motives of politicians and so-called leaders. When the parties they supported were in power, they would push the demons back. When their opponents came to power, they would again summon up this unholy alliance as the reason why Blacks could make no progress. Well, I am here to say that discrimination, racism, and bigotry have gone no place and probably never will. What does that mean for us—for you graduates? Does it mean that you roll over and give up? Does it mean you do nothing until these hideous creatures of hate are destroyed? Does it mean you accept no responsibility for your future? For your lives?

You know, in 1964, when I entered the Seminary on the Isle of Hope, I was the only Black in my class and one of two in the school. A year later, I was the only one in the school. Not a day passed that I was not pricked by that ever-present trident of prejudice.

But I had an advantage over Black students and kids today, I had never heard any excuses made. Nor had I seen my role models take comfort in excuses. The women who worked in those kitchens and waited on the bus knew it was prejudice which caused their plight, but that didn't stop them from working. My grandfather knew why his business wasn't more successful, but that didn't stop him from getting up at two in the morning to carry ice, wood, and fuel oil. Sure, they knew it was bad. They knew all too well that they were held back by prejudice. But they weren't pinned down by it. They fought against discrimination under the leadership of W. W. Law and the NAACP. Equally important, they fought against the awful effects of prejudice by doing all they could do in spite of this obstacle. They could still send their children to school, they could still respect and help each other, they could still moderate their use of alcohol; they could still be decent, law-abiding citizens. I had the benefit of people who knew they had to walk a straighter line, climb a taller mountain, and carry a heavier load. They took all that segregation and prejudice would allow them *and* at the same time fought to remove these awful barriers.

You all have a much tougher road to travel. Not only do you have to contend with the ever-present bigotry, you must do so with a recent tradition that almost requires you to wallow in excuses. You now have a popular national rhetoric which says that you can't learn because of racism, you can't raise the babies you make because of racism, you can't get up in the mornings because of racism. You commit crimes because of racism. Unlike me you must not only overcome the repressiveness of racism, you must also overcome the lure of excuses. You have twice the job I had.

In Greek mythology, sirens with their bewitching sweetness, lured ships to their destruction on dangerous rocky coastlines. There will be many, many such sirens in your lives. They will attempt to lure you to the rocks of certain destruction and definite failure. They will try to convince you that others have total control over your lives—that politicians here, in Atlanta, and in Washington have more to do with your success than you do.

They don't. Do not be lured by their sirens and purveyors of misery who profit from constantly regurgitating all that is wrong with Black Americans and blaming these problems on others. Do not succumb to this temptation of always blaming others. Do not become obsessed with all that is wrong with our race. Rather, become obsessed with looking for solutions to our problems. Be tolerant of all positive ideas, their number is much smaller than the countless number of problems to be solved. We need *all* the hope we can get.

Most importantly, draw on that great lesson and those positive role models who have gone down this road before us. We are badgered and pushed by our friends and peers to do unlike our parents and grandparents—we are told not to be old fashioned. But they have weathered the storm. It is up to us now to learn how. Countless hours of research are spent to determine why Blacks fail or why we commit crimes. Why can't we spend a few hours learning how those closest to us have survived and helped us get this far? As your frontrunner, I have gone ahead and taken a long, hard look. I have seen two roads from my perch a few humble feet above the maddening crowd. On the first, a race of people is rushing mindlessly down a highway of sweet, intoxicating destruction, with all its bright lights and grand promises, constructed by social scientists and politicians. To the side, there is a seldom used, overgrown road leading through the valley of life with all its pitfalls and obstacles, with all its hatred and discrimination. It is a difficult "winding, meandering" road, full of ups and downs, with no promise of certain success. But it is a road of hope and opportunity. It is the road—the old fashioned road—travelled by those who endured slavery—who endured Jim Crowism—who endured hatred. It is the road that *might* reward hard work and discipline; that *might* reward intelligence; that *might* be fair and provide equal opportunity. But there are no guarantees.

You must choose. The lure of the highway is seductive and enticing, but the destruction is certain. To travel the road of hope and opportunity is hard and difficult, but there is a chance that you might somehow, someway, with the help of God— make it!

Two decades from now you must face your children and other graduates who must choose. Will you say I was destroyed by the fast life of the fast highway, or will you be able to say in the words of Robert Frost:

"Two roads diverged in the woods, and I—I took the one less travelled by, and that has made all the difference."

The roads are there. The challenge is clear. The choice is yours. I wish you good luck and Godspeed!

❏

I   n his opening statement on Sept. 10, 1991, at the first round of confirmation hearings before the Senate Committee on the Judiciary, Clarence Thomas provided more insight into the early life experiences that helped shape his views.

❑

TESTIMONY OF HON. CLARENCE THOMAS, OF GEORGIA, TO BE ASSOCIATE JUSTICE OF THE UNITED STATES SUPREME COURT

Judge THOMAS. Mr. Chairman, Senator Thurmond, members of the Committee, I am humbled and honored to have been nominated by President Bush to be an Associate Justice of the Supreme Court of the United States. . . .

My earliest memories, as alluded to earlier, are those of Pin Point, Georgia, a life far removed in space and time from this room, this day and this moment. As kids, we caught minnows in the creeks, fidler [sic] crabs in the marshes, we played with pluffers [sic], and skipped shells across the water. It was a world so vastly different from all this.

In 1955, my brother and I went to live with my mother in Savannah. We lived in one room in a tenement. We shared a kitchen with other tenants and we had a common bathroom in the backyard which was unworkable and unusable. It was hard, but it was all we had and all there was.

Our mother only earned $20 every two weeks as a maid, not enough to take care of us. So she arranged for us to live with our grandparents later, in 1955. Imagine, if you will, two little boys with all their belongings in two grocery bags.

Our grandparents were two great and wonderful people who loved us dearly. I wish they were sitting here today. Sitting here so they could see that all their efforts, their hard work were not in vain, and so that they could see that hard work and strong values can make for a better life. . . .

I attended segregated parochial schools and later attended a seminary near Savannah. The nuns gave us hope and belief in ourselves when society didn't. They reinforced the importance of religious beliefs in our personal lives. Sister Mary Virgilius, my eighth grade teacher, and the other nuns were unyielding in their expectations that we use all of our talents no matter what the rest of the world said or did.

After high school, I left Savannah and attended Immaculate Conception Seminary, then Holy Cross College. I attended Yale Law School. Yale had opened its doors, its heart, its conscience to recruit and admit minority students. I benefitted from this effort. . . .

I was an Assistant Attorney General in the State of Missouri. I was an attorney in the corporate law department of Monsanto Company. I joined Senator Danforth's staff here in the Senate, was an Assistant Secretary in the Department of Education, Chairman of EEOC, and since 1990 a judge on the U.S. Court of Appeals for the District of Columbia Circuit.

But for the efforts of so many others who have gone before me, I would not be here today. It would be unimaginable. Only by standing on their shoulders could I be here. At each turn in my life, each obstacle confronted, each fork in the road, someone came along to help.

I remember, for example, in 1974 after I completed law school I had no money, no place to live. Mrs. Margaret Bush Wilson, who would later become chairperson of the NAACP, allowed me to live at her house. She provided me not only with room and board, but advice, counsel and guidance. . . .

Justice Marshall, whose seat I have been nominated to fill, is one of those who had the courage and the intellect. He is one of the great architects of the legal battles to open doors that seemed so hopelessly and permanently sealed and to knock down barriers that seemed so insurmountable to those of us in the Pin Point, Georgias of the world.

The civil rights movement, Reverent [sic] Martin Luther King and the SCLC, Roy Wilkins and the NAACP, Whitney Young and the Urban League, Fannie Lou Haemer, Rosa Parks and Dorothy Hite, they changed society and made it reach out and affirmatively help. I have benefited greatly from their efforts. But for them there would have been no road to travel.

My grandparents always said there would be more opportunities for us. I can still hear my grandfather, "Y'all goin' have mo' of a chance then me," and he was right. He felt that if others sacrificed and created opportunities for us we had an obligation to work hard, to be decent citizens, to be fair and good people, and he was right.

. . . I have always carried in my heart the world, the life, the people, the values of my youth, the values of my grandparents and my neighbors, the values of people who believed so very deeply in this country in spite of all the contradictions.

It is my hope that when these hearings are completed that this committee will conclude that I am an honest, decent, fair person. I believe that the obligations and responsibilities of a judge, in essence, involve just such basic values. A judge must be fair and impartial. A judge must not bring to his job, to the court, the baggage of preconceived notions, of ideology, and certainly not an agenda, and the judge must get the decision right. Because when all is said and done, the little guy, the average person, the people of Pin Point, the real people of America will be affected not only by what we as judges do, but by the way we do our jobs.

If confirmed by the Senate I pledge that I will preserve and protect our Constitution and carry with me the values of my heritage: fairness, integrity, open-mindedness, honesty, and hard work.

❏

J *ustice Thomas was the first witness to testify at the*
second round of hearings, which began on October 11, 1991.

❑

TESTIMONY OF HON. CLARENCE THOMAS, OF GEORGIA, TO BE
ASSOCIATE JUSTICE OF THE U.S. SUPREME COURT

Judge THOMAS. Mr. Chairman, Senator Thurmond, members
of the committee:

As excruciatingly difficult as the last 2 weeks have been, I
welcome the opportunity to clear my name today. No one other
than my wife and Senator Danforth, to whom I read this statement at 6:30 A.M., has seen or heard the statement, no handlers,
no advisors.

The first I learned of the allegations by Prof. Anita Hill was
on September 25, 1991, when the FBI came to my home to
investigate her allegations. When informed by the FBI agent of
the nature of the allegations and the person making them, I was
shocked, surprised, hurt and enormously saddened.

I have not been the same since that day. For almost a decade
my responsibilities included enforcing the rights of victims of
sexual harassment. As a boss, as a friend, and as a human being
I was proud that I have never had such an allegation leveled
against me, even as I sought to promote women, and minorities
into nontraditional jobs.

In addition, several of my friends, who are women, have
confided in me about the horror of harassment on the job, or
elsewhere. I thought I really understood the anguish, the fears,
the doubts, the seriousness of the matter. But since September
25, I have suffered immensely as these very serious charges
were leveled against me.

I have been racking my brains, and eating my insides out trying to think of what I could have said or done to Anita Hill to lead her to allege that I was interested in her in more than a professional way, and that I talked with her about pornographic or X-rated films.

Contrary to some press reports, I categorically denied all of the allegations and denied that I ever attempted to date Anita Hill, when first interviewed by the FBI. I strongly reaffirm that denial. Let me describe my relationship with Anita Hill.

In 1981, after I went to the Department of Education as an Assistant Secretary in the Office of Civil Rights, one of my closest friends, from both college and law school, Gil Hardy, brought Anita Hill to my attention. As I remember, he indicated that she was dissatisfied with her law firm and wanted to work in government. Based primarily, if not solely, on Gil's recommendation, I hired Anita Hill.

During my tenure at the Department of Education, Anita Hill was an attorney-advisor who worked directly with me. She worked on special projects, as well as day-to-day matters. As I recall, she was one of two professionals working directly with me at the time. As a result, we worked closely on numerous matters.

I recall being pleased with her work product and the professional, but cordial relationship which we enjoyed at work. I also recall engaging in discussions about politics and current events.

Upon my nomination to become Chairman of the Equal Employment Opportunity Commission, Anita Hill, to the best of my recollection, assisted me in the nomination and confirmation process. After my confirmation, she and Diane Holt, then my secretary, joined me at EEOC. I do not recall that there was any question or doubts that she would become a special assistant to me at EEOC, although as a career employee she retained the option of remaining at the Department of Education.

At EEOC our relationship was more distant. And our

contacts less frequent, as a result of the increased size of my personal staff and the dramatic increase and diversity of my day-to-day responsibilities.

Upon reflection, I recall that she seemed to have had some difficulty adjusting to this change in her role. In any case, our relationship remained both cordial and professional. At no time did I become aware, either directly or indirectly that she felt I had said, or done anything to change the cordial nature of our relationship.

I detected nothing from her or from my staff, or from Gil Hardy, our mutual friend, with whom I maintained regular contact. I am certain that had any statement or conduct on my part been brought to my attention, I would remember it clearly because of the nature and seriousness of such conduct, as well as my adamant opposition to sex discrimination sexual harassment.

But there were no such statements.

In the spring of 1983, Mr. Charles Cothey [sic] contacted me to speak at the law school at Oral Roberts University in Tulsa, OK. Anita Hill, who is from Oklahoma, accompanied me on that trip. It was not unusual that individuals on my staff would travel with me occasionally. Anita Hill accompanied me on that trip primarily because this was an opportunity to combine business and a visit to her home.

As I recall, during our visit at Oral Roberts University, Mr. Cothey [sic] mentioned to me the possibility of approaching Anita Hill to join the faculty at Oral Roberts University Law School. I encouraged him to do so. I noted to him, as I recall, that Anita Hill would do well in teaching. I recommended her highly and she eventually was offered a teaching position.

Although I did not see Anita Hill often after she left EEOC, I did see her on one or two subsequent visits to Tulsa, OK. And on one visit I believe she drove me to the airport. I also occasionally received telephone calls from her. She would speak directly with me or with my secretary, Diane Holt. Since Anita

Hill and Diane Holt had been with me at the Department of Education they were fairly close personally and I believe they occasionally socialized together.

I would also hear about her through Linda Jackson, then Linda Lambert, whom both Anita Hill and I met at the Department of Education. And I would hear of her from my friend Gil.

Throughout the time that Anita Hill worked with me I treated her as I treated my other special assistants. I tried to treat them all cordially, professionally, and respectfully. And I tried to support them in their endeavors, and be interested in and supportive of their success.

I had no reason or basis to believe my relationship with Anita Hill was anything but this way until the FBI visited me a little more than two weeks ago. I find it particularly troubling that she never raised any hint that she was uncomfortable with me. She did not raise or mention it when considering moving with me to EEOC from the Department of Education. And she never raised it with me when she left EEOC and was moving on in her life.

And to my fullest knowledge, she did not speak to any other women working with or around me, who would feel comfortable enough to raise it with me, especially Diane Holt, to whom she seemed closest on my personal staff. Nor did she raise it with mutual friends, such as Linda Jackson, and Gil Hardy.

This is a person I have helped at every turn in the road, since we met. She seemed to appreciate the continued cordial relationship we had since day one. She sought my advice and counsel, as did virtually all of the members of my personal staff.

During my tenure in the executive branch as a manager, as a policymaker and as a person, I have adamantly condemned sex harassment. There is no member of this committee or this Senate who feels stronger about sex harassment than I do. As a manager, I made every effort to take swift and decisive action when sex harassment raised or reared its ugly head.

The fact that I feel so very strongly about sex harassment and spoke loudly about it at EEOC has made these allegations doubly hard on me. I cannot imagine anything that I said or did to Anita Hill that could have been mistaken for sexual harassment.

But with that said, if there is anything that I have said that has been misconstrued by Anita Hill or anyone else, to be sexually [sic] harassment, then I can say that I am so very sorry and I wish I had known. If I did know I would have stopped immediately and I would not, as I have done over the past 2 weeks, had to tear away at myself trying to think of what I could possibly have done. But I have not said or done the things that Anita Hill has alleged.

God has gotten me through the days since September 25 and He is my judge.

Mr. Chairman, something has happened to me in the dark days that have followed since the FBI agents informed me about these allegations. And the days have grown darker, as this very serious, very explosive, and very sensitive allegation or these sensitive allegations were selectively leaked, in a distorted way to the media over the past weekend.

As if the confidential allegations, themselves, were not enough, this apparently calculated public disclosure has caused me, my family, and my friends enormous pain and great harm.

I have never, in all my life, felt such hurt, such pain, such agony. My family and I have been done a grave and irreparable injustice. During the past 2 weeks, I lost the belief that if I did my best all would work out. I called upon the strength that helped me get here from Pin Point, and it was all sapped out of me. It was sapped out of me because Anita Hill was a person I considered a friend, whom I admired and thought I had treated fairly and with the utmost respect. Perhaps I could have better weathered this if it were from someone else, but here was someone I truly felt I had done my best with.

Though I am, by no means, a perfect person, no means, I have not done what she has alleged, and I still do not know what I could possibly have done to cause her to make these allegations.

When I stood next to the President in Kennebunkport, being nominated to the Supreme Court of the United States, that was a high honor. But as I sit here, before you, 103 days later, that honor has been crushed. From the very beginning charges were leveled against me from the shadows—charges of drug abuse, antisemitism [sic], wife-beating, drug use by family members, that I was a quota appointment, confirmation conversion and much, much more, and now, this.

I have complied with the rules. I responded to a document request that produced over 30,000 pages of documents. And I have testified for 5 full days, under oath. I have endured this ordeal for 103 days. Reporters sneaking into my garage to examine books I read. Reporters and interest groups swarming over divorce papers, looking for dirt. Unnamed people starting preposterous and damaging rumors. Calls all over the country specifically requesting dirt. This is not American. This is Kafka-esque. It has got to stop. It must stop for the benefit of future nominees, and our country. Enough is enough.

I am not going to allow myself to be further humiliated in order to be confirmed. I am here specifically to respond to allegations of sex harassment in the work place. I am not here to be further humiliated by this committee, or anyone else, or to put my private life on display for a prurient interest or other reasons. I will not allow this committee or anyone else to probe into my private life. This is not what America is all about.

To ask me to do that would be to ask me to go beyond fundamental fairness. Yesterday, I called my mother. She was confined to her bed, unable to work and unable to stop crying. Enough is enough.

Mr. Chairman, in my 43 years on this Earth, I have been able, with the help of others and with the help of God, to defy poverty, avoid prison, overcome segregation, bigotry, racism, and obtain one of the finest educations available in this country.

But I have not been able to overcome this process. This is worse than any obstacle or anything that I have ever faced. Throughout my life I have been energized by the expectation and the hope that in this country I would be treated fairly in all endeavors. When there was segregation I hoped there would be fairness one day or some day. When there was bigotry and prejudice I hoped that there would be tolerance and understanding some day.

Mr. Chairman, I am proud of my life, proud of what I have done, and what I have accomplished, proud of my family, and this process, this process is trying to destroy it all. No job is worth what I have been through, no job. No horror in my life has been so debilitating. Confirm me if you want, don't confirm me if you are so led, but let this process end. Let me and my family regain our lives. I never asked to be nominated. It was an honor. Little did I know the price, but it is too high.

I enjoy and appreciate my current position, and I am comfortable with the prospect of returning to my work as a judge on the U.S. Court of Appeals for the D.C. Circuit and to my friends there.

Each of these positions is public service, and I have given at the office. I want my life and my family's life back and I want them returned expeditiously.

I have experienced the exhilaration of new heights from the moment I was called to Kennebunkport by the President to have lunch and he nominated me. That was the high point. At that time I was told eye-to-eye that, Clarence, you made it this far on merit, the rest is going to be politics and it surely has been. There have been other highs. The outpouring of support from my friends of long-standing, a bonding like I have never experienced with my old boss, Senator Danforth, the wonderful support of those who have worked with me.

There have been prayers said for my family, and me, by people I know and people I will never meet, prayers that were heard and that sustained not only me, but also my wife and my entire family. Instead of understanding and appreciating the great honor bestowed upon me, I find myself, here today defending my name, my integrity, because somehow select portions of confidential documents, dealing with this matter were leaked to the public.

Mr. Chairman, I am a victim of this process and my name has been harmed, my integrity has been harmed, my character has been harmed, my family has been harmed, my friends have been harmed. There is nothing this committee, this body or this country can do to give me my good name back, nothing.

I will not provide the rope for my own lynching or for further humiliation. I am not going to engage in discussions, nor will I submit to roving questions of what goes on in the most intimate parts of my private live [sic] or the sanctity of my bedroom. These are the most intimate parts of my privacy, and they will remain just that, private.

❑

*J*ustice Thomas initially was scheduled to respond to questions immediately after his opening statement. However, because the Judiciary Committee had not yet resolved Anita Hill's request to keep confidential a statement containing some of her allegations, Justice Thomas was excused temporarily and Ms. Hill called instead as the first witness.

Consequently, when he returned later to answer questions, Clarence Thomas had the opportunity to make additional opening remarks.

❏

FURTHER TESTIMONY OF HON. CLARENCE THOMAS, OF GEORGIA, TO BE ASSOCIATE JUSTICE OF THE UNITED STATES SUPREME COURT

The CHAIRMAN [JOSEPH R. BIDEN, JR.]. Do you have anything you would like to say?

Judge THOMAS. Senator, I would like to start by saying unequivocally, uncategorically that I deny each and every single allegation against me today that suggested in any way that I had conversations of a sexual nature or about pornographic material with Anita Hill, that I ever attempted to date her, that I ever had any personal sexual interest in her, or that I in any way ever harassed her.

Second, and I think a more important point, I think that this today is a travesty. I think that it is disgusting. I think that this hearing should never occur in America. This is a case in which this sleaze, this dirt was searched for by staffers of members of this committee, was then leaked to the media, and this committee and this body validated it and displayed it in prime time over our entire Nation.

How would any member on this committee or any person in this room or any person in this country like sleaze said about him or her in this fashion or this dirt dredged up and this gossip and these lies displayed in this manner? How would any person like it?

The Supreme Court is not worth it. No job is worth it. I am not here for that. I am here for my name, my family, my life and my integrity. I think something is dreadfully wrong with this country, when any person, any person in this free country would be subjected to this. This is not a closed room.

There was an FBI investigation. This is not an opportunity to talk about difficult matters privately or in a closed environment. This is a circus. It is as [sic] national disgrace. And from my standpoint, as a black American, as far as I am concerned, it is a high-tech lynching for uppity-blacks who in any way deign to think for themselves, to do for themselves, to have different ideas, and it is a message that, unless you kow-tow to an old order, this is what will happen to you, you will be lynched, destroyed, caricatured by a committee of the U.S. Senate, rather than hung from a tree.

❑

$\boxed{S}$ *enator Charles E. Grassley later asked witness Nancy E. Fitch, an associate professor of African-American studies and an historian, to elaborate on Justice Thomas' comment on lynching during his second opening statement.*

❏

Senator GRASSLEY. Okay, I guess the only thing I would do and this is from your expertise as a historian, Professor Fitch, I wondered if I might ask you to draw on that background for a moment and you heard Friday Judge Thomas testify that he compared his treatment here to a lynching. I would like to have you explain or elaborate that comparison for us.

Why is this ordeal, defending against a charge of sex harassment similar to a lynching, as he put it?

Ms. FITCH. I haven't talked to the Judge since he made those comments, but when he made those comments I felt that I understood them. I have a student who is working on lynching right now, so I have been thinking about this. Lynching was something that was done to intimate [sic] people, that was done to control them, as well as kill them. And I think, if I understand what the Judge was saying, was that this was an attempt to do that to him; that the process, the subsequent confirmation hearings process, this process was patently unfair, that it was a way to neutralize and control and intimidate not just him, but possibly through him, any person that was considered, as he put it, uppity.

When black soldiers came back from World War I, they felt that they had proved themselves to the country and to their fellow citizens. And wore their uniforms down south and that was a sure way to get yourself lynched, because they were wrapped, so to speak, in the American flag. That was to tell these people that they were not Americans. I see a connection and understood what he meant by that. He said, electronic lynching, I believe.

Senator GRASSLEY. Well, do you sense that then there has to be a larger group of people that see him a threat or people who think like him as a threat and they have to be put down right now or what will happen if they are not put down right now?

Ms. FITCH. Senator, I have talked to a colleague who worked with us on personal staff who you may have a statement from, I am not sure, and we talked about this on the phone and his words, subsequently, I think used in the press were character assassination. For me the operative word there is assassination. And the other word is neutralization and I felt and some of us do feel that any person of color in this country who goes against the stream of what people think black people in this country should be thinking and feeling and doing by so distinguishing themselves, put themselves at great risk. . . .

❑

Further along in the proceedings, witness Phyllis Berry[-Myers] offered another perspective.

Senator [HERBERT] KOHL. . . . Clarence Thomas has spoken here of a conspiracy, a lynching conspiracy on the part of some white people that have a lot to do with what is happening. . . . But isn't it a fact that what we are dealing with here is a charge of sexual harassment by a black African-American against an African-American? Isn't that why we are here today? Isn't that the fact of what brings us here today, an African-American woman who is charging an African-American man with sexual harassment? Is there something else that brings us here today?

I mean we are all here and we had to take a car to get here, and there was a Senate committee that is convening to hold this hearing, but it is caused by what other than a charge leveled at an African man by an African woman?

Ms. BERRY. That's an old tactic in this country, Senator, that we use and I am sickened by that. That's the thing, I guess, that embarrasses me most about this situation is that a black woman would allow herself to be a pawn to destroy a black man. Have we reached the point in our civilization or in this country where people can't legitimately have points of disagreement without trying to destroy the person because you don't agree with what that person stands for.

❑

E xcerpts *from the Senators' questions and Justice Thomas' answers follow:*

❑

Senator [HOWELL] HEFLIN. . . . Now, I suppose you have heard Professor Hill, Ms. Hill, Anita F. Hill testify today.
Judge THOMAS. No, I haven't.
Senator HEFLIN. You didn't listen?
Judge THOMAS. No, I didn't. I have heard enough lies.
Senator HEFLIN. You didn't listen to her testimony?
Judge THOMAS. No, I didn't.
Senator HEFLIN. On television?
Judge THOMAS. No, I didn't. I've heard enough lies. Today is not a day that, in my opinion, is high among the days in our country. This is a travesty. You spent the entire day destroying what it has taken me 43 years to build and providing a forum for that.
Senator HEFLIN. Judge Thomas, you know we have a responsibility too, and as far as I am involved, I had nothing to do with Anita Hill coming here and testifying. We are trying to get to the bottom of this. And, if she is lying, then I think you can help us prove that she was lying.
Judge THOMAS. Senator, I am incapable of proving the negative that did not occur.
Senator HEFLIN. Well, if it did not occur, I think you are in a position, with certainly your ability to testify, in effect, to try to eliminate it from people's minds.
Judge THOMAS. Senator, I didn't create it in people's minds. This matter was investigated by the Federal Bureau of Investigation in a confidential way. It was then leaked last weekend to the media. I did not do that. And how many members of this

Committee would like to have the same scurrilous, uncorrobo-
rated allegations made about him and then leaked to national
newspapers and then be drawn and dragged before a national
forum of this nature to discuss those allegations that should
have been resolved in a confidential way?

Senator HEFLIN. Well, I certainly appreciate your attitude
towards leaks. I happen to serve on the Senate Ethics Committee and it has been a sieve.

Judge THOMAS. But it didn't leak on me. This leaked on me
and it is drowning my life, my career and my integrity, and you
can't give it back to me, and this Committee can't give it back to
me, and this Senate can't give it back to me. You have robbed me
of something that can never be restored.

Senator [DENNIS] DeCONCINI. I know exactly how you feel.

❏

*Later in the proceedings, Senator Arlen Specter also ques-
tioned Justice Thomas about his decision not to listen to Anita
Hill's testimony.*

Senator SPECTER. Judge Thomas, I was a little disappointed,
maybe more than a little disappointed, that you did not watch
the proceedings yesterday, in terms of seeing precisely what
Professor Hill had to say, both from the point of view of wanting
to know what it was and from the point of view of being in a
better position to defend yourself. Why didn't you watch those
hearings?

Judge THOMAS. Senator, the last two and a half weeks have
been a living hell and there is only so much a human being can
take, and as far as I was concerned, the statements that she sent
to this committee and her statements to the FBI were lies and
they were untrue, and I didn't see any reason to suffer through
more lies about me. This is not an easy experience.

Senator SPECTER. Judge Thomas, I can understand that it

is not an easy experience for you. It hasn't been an easy experience for anybody. But in the context where she comes forward and she is testifying, and the fact is she said much more in her statement here than she had in either her written statement to the committee on September 23rd or what she said to the FBI, and there was as good bit of exchange above and beyond what she said, and it just struck me a little peculiarly that you had not wanted to see what she had said, realizing the difficulty, but also focusing on the question of being able to respond. It is a little hard to ask you questions, if you haven't seen her testimony. It requires going through a lot of the record. I just was concerned that you had taken that course, in light of the seriousness, the importance and the gravity of the matter.

Judge THOMAS. Senator, I wish there was more for me to give, but I have given all I can.

❑

Senator HATCH. Judge Thomas, I have sat here and I have listened all day long, and Anita Hill was very impressive. She is an impressive law professor. She is a Yale Law graduate. And, when she met with the FBI, she said that you told her about your sexual experiences and preferences. And I hate to go into this but I want to go into it because I have to, and I know that it is something that you wish you had never heard at any time or place. But I think it is important that we go into it and let me just do it this way.

She said to the FBI that you told her about your sexual experiences and preferences, that you asked her what she liked or if she had ever done the same thing, that you discussed oral sex between men and women, that you discussed viewing films of people having sex with each other and with animals, and that you told her that she should see such films, and that you would like to discuss specific sex acts and the frequency of sex.

What about that?

Judge THOMAS. Senator, I would not want to, except being required to here, to dignify those allegations with a response. As I have said before, I categorically deny them. To me, I have been pilloried with scurrilous allegations of this nature. I have denied them earlier and I deny them tonight.

Senator HATCH. Judge Thomas, today in a new statement in addition to what she had told the FBI, which I have to agree with you is quite a bit, she made a number of other allegations and what I would like to do is—some of them most specifically were for the first time today in addition to these, which I think almost anybody would say are terrible. And I would just like to give you an opportunity, because this is your chance to address her testimony.

At any time did you say to Professor Hill that she could ruin your career if she talked about sexual comments you allegedly made to her?

Judge THOMAS. No.

Senator HATCH. Did you say to her in words or substance that you could ruin her career?

Judge THOMAS. No.

Senator HATCH. Should she ever have been afraid of you and any kind of vindictiveness to ruin her career?

Judge THOMAS. Senator, I have made it my business to help my Special Assistants. I recommended Ms. Hill for her position at Oral Roberts University. I have always spoken highly of her.

I had no reason prior to the FBI visiting me a little more than 2 weeks ago to know that she harbored any ill feelings toward me or any discomfort with me. This is all new to me.

Senator HATCH. It is new to me too, because I read the FBI report at least 10 or 15 times. I didn't see any of these allegations I am about to go into, including that one. But she seemed to sure have a recollection here today.

Now, did you ever say to Professor Hill in words or substance, and this is embarrassing for me to say in public, but it has to be done, and I am sure it is not pleasing to you.

Did you ever say in words or substance something like there is a pubic hair in my coke?

Judge THOMAS. No, Senator.

Senator HATCH. Did you ever refer to your private parts in conversations with Professor Hill?

Judge THOMAS. Absolutely not, Senator.

Senator HATCH. Did you ever brag to Professor Hill about your sexual prowess?

Judge THOMAS. No, Senator.

Senator HATCH. Did you ever use the term "Long Dong Silver" in conversation with Professor Hill?

Judge THOMAS. No, Senator.

Senator HATCH. Did you ever have lunch with Professor Hill at which you talked about sex or pressured her to go out with you?

Judge THOMAS. Absolutely not.

Senator HATCH. Did you ever tell—

Judge THOMAS. [continuing]. I have had no such discussions, nor have I ever pressured or asked her to go out with me beyond her work environment.

Senator HATCH. Did you ever tell Professor Hill that she should see pornographic films?

Judge THOMAS. Absolutely not.

Senator HATCH. Did you ever talk about pornography with Professor Hill?

Judge THOMAS. I did not discuss any pornographic material or pornographic preferences or pornographic films with Professor Hill.

Senator HATCH. So you never even talked or described pornographic materials with her?

Judge THOMAS. Absolutely not.

Senator HATCH. Amongst those or in addition?

Judge THOMAS. What I have told you is precisely what I told

the FBI on September 25 when they shocked me with the allegations made by Anita Hill.

Senator HATCH. . . . Let me ask you something. You have dealt with these problems for a long time. At one time I was the Chairman of reviewing the EEOC and, I might add, the Department of Education, and I am the ranking member today, and I have known you for 11 years and you are an expert. Because you are the person who made the arguments to then Solicitor General Fried that the Administration should strongly take a position on sexual harassment cases in the *Meritor Savings Bank* v. *Vinson* case, and the Supreme Court adopted your position.

Did I misstate that?

Judge THOMAS. Senator, what you have said is substantially accurate. What I attempted to do in my discussions with the Solicitor is to have them be aggressive in that litigation, and EEOC was very instrumental in the success in the *Meritor* case.

❑

Senator Hatch later pointed out that, in addition to taking a leading role in establishing the government's position against sexual harassment in Meritor Savings Bank v. Vinson, *Justice Thomas enforced stringent prohibitions against sexual harassment at the Equal Employment Opportunity Commission when he was chairman.*

Senator HATCH. . . . Judge Thomas, I have a copy of a November 14, 1984, memorandum concerning sexual harassment that you issued within the EEOC. The memo emphasizes the importance of an earlier EEOC order issued shortly before your arrival at that agency.

Judge Thomas, before I get into that memo, I would just like to say this to you, and I wrote it down, because I wanted to say it right: I have to tell you, Judge Thomas, I have reflected on these hearings—this is my handwriting—and what has unfolded this past week is terrible. One of the things that I find most ironic is that many have tried to turn this issue into a referendum on sexual harassment.

Well, let me say, this is not a referendum on sexual harassment. We all deplore sexual harassment. We all deplore the type of conduct articulated here by Professor Hill. But the most ironic thing to me is, it is easy for us on this committee to say that we deplore sexual harassment, and many on this committee have said in the past and during these proceedings and before the media.

But you, Judge Thomas you have spent your career doing something about it, a heck of a lot more than deploring sexual harassment. You and your people at the EEOC have been directly involved and have done a lot about it, I know that, because, along with Senator Kennedy and the other members of the Labor Committee, we oversee what you do.

Now, the memo that you issued at the EEOC on sexual harassment, this emphasizes the importance of an earlier EEOC order issued shortly before your arrival at the agency, and that memo stated in unequivocal terms that sexual harassment is illegal.

The final paragraph of the memo, which was signed by you, reads as follows:

I expect every Commission employee to personally insure that their own conduct does not sexually harass other employees, applicants or any other individual in the workplace. Managers are to take the strongest disciplinary measure against those employees found guilty of sexual harassment. Sexual harassment will not be tolerated at the agency.

Underlined.

Now, Judge Thomas, does this memo reflect a major policy commitment of yours?

Judge THOMAS. It expresses my strong attitude and my adamant attitude that sex harassment was not to take place at EEOC.

Senator HATCH. Judge Thomas, I also have a copy of an EEOC plan for the prevention of sexual harassment issued in 1987, while you were Chairman of the Equal Employment Opportunity Commission, which clearly states that sexual harassment includes "unwelcome sexual teasing, jokes, remarks or questions." Now, is this consistent with the views that you personally have believed in and have abided by during your lifetime?

Judge THOMAS. Yes.

Senator HATCH. Or certainly during these last 10 or 11 years—

Judge THOMAS. Yes, Senator.

Senator HATCH [continuing]. Which are the years in question. Was sexual harassment tolerated within the EEOC by you, as Chairman, or while you were Chairman?

Judge THOMAS. Absolutely not.

❑

Judge THOMAS. Well, the difficulty also was that, from my standpoint, is that in this country when it comes to sexual conduct we still have underlying racial attitudes about black men and their views of sex. And once you pin that on me, I can't get it off. That is why I am so adamant in this committee about what has been done to me. I made it a point at EEOC and at Education not to play into those stereotypes, at all. I made it a point to have the people at those agencies, the black men, the black women to conduct themselves in a way that is not consistent with those stereotypes, and I did the same thing myself.

❑

Senator HATCH. . . . Now, I want to ask you about this intriguing thing you just said. You said some of this language is stereotype language? What does that mean, I don't understand.

Judge THOMAS. Senator, the language throughout the history of this country, and certainly throughout my life, language about the sexual prowess of black men, language about the sex organs of black men, and the sizes, et cetera, that kind of language has been used about black men as long as I have been on the face of this Earth. These are charges that play into racist, bigoted stereotypes and these are the kind of charges that are impossible to wash off. And these are the kinds of stereotypes that I have, in my tenure in Government, and the conduct of my affairs, attempted to move away from and to convince people that we should conduct ourselves in a way that defies these stereotypes. But when you play into a stereotype it is as though you are skiing downhill, there's no way to stop it.

And this plays into the most bigoted, racist stereotypes that any black man will face.

Senator HATCH. Well, I saw—I didn't understand the television program, there were two black men—I may have it wrong, but as I recall—there were two black men talking about this matter and one of them said, she is trying to demonize us. I didn't understand it at the time. Do you understand that?

Judge THOMAS. Well, I understand it and any black man in this country—Senator, in the 1970's I became very interested in the issue of lynching. And if you want to track through this country, in the 19th and 20th century, the lynchings of black men, you will see that there is invariably or in many instances a relationship with sex—an accusation that that person cannot shake off. That is the point that I am trying to make. And that is the point that I was making last night that this is high-tech lynching. I cannot shake off these accusations because they play to the worst stereotypes we have about black men in this country.

Senator HATCH. Well, this bothers me.

Judge THOMAS. It bothers me.

Senator HATCH. I can see why. Let me, I hate to do this, but let me ask you some tough questions. You have talked about stereotypes used against black males in this society. In this first statement he told her about his experiences and preferences and would ask her what she liked or if she had ever done the same thing? Is that a black stereotype?

Judge THOMAS. No.

Senator HATCH. OK. Hill said that he discussed oral sex between men and women. Is that a black stereotype?

Judge THOMAS. No.

Senator HATCH. Thomas also discussed viewing films of people having sex with each other and with animals. What about that?

Judge THOMAS. That's not a stereotype about blacks.

Senator HATCH. OK. He told her that he enjoyed watching the films and told her that she should see them. Watching X-rated films or pornographic films, is that a stereotype?

Judge THOMAS. No.

Senator HATCH. He never asked her to watch the films with him. Thomas liked to discuss specific sex acts and frequency of sex.

Judge THOMAS. No, I don't think so. I think that could—the last, frequency—could have to do with black men supposedly being very promiscuous or something like that.

Senator HATCH. So it could be partially stereotypical?

Judge THOMAS. Yes.

Senator HATCH. In the next statement she said,

His conversations were very vivid. He spoke about acts that he had seen in pornographic films involving such things as women having sex with animals and films involving group sex or rape scenes. He talked about pornographic materials depicting individuals with large penises or breasts involved in various sex acts.

What about those things?

Judge THOMAS. I think certainly the size of sexual organs would be something.

Senator HATCH. Well, I am concerned. "Thomas told me graphically of his own sexual prowess", the third statement.

Judge THOMAS. That is clearly—

Senator HATCH. Clearly a black stereotype.

Judge THOMAS [continuing]. Stereotypical, clearly.

Senator HATCH. Do you think that—well, what do you feel about that?

Judge THOMAS. Senator, as I have said before, this whole affair has been anguish for me. I feel as though I have been abused in this process, as I said last night, and I continue to feel that way. I feel as though something has been lodged against me and painted on me and it will leave an indelible mark on me. This is something that not only supports but plays into the worst stereotypes about black men in this society. And I have no way of changing it, and no way of refuting these charges.

Senator HATCH. Now, let me just—people hearing yesterday's testimony are probably wondering how could this quiet, you know, retired, woman know about something like "Long Dong Silver"? Did you tell her that?

Judge THOMAS. No, I don't know how she knows.

Senator HATCH. Is that a black stereotype, something like Long Dong Silver?

Judge THOMAS. To the extent, Senator, that it is a reference to one's sexual organs, and the size of one's sexual organs, I think it is.

◻

Later, Senator Hatch asked Dr. Fitch about the stereotypes to which Justice Thomas referred.

Senator HATCH. Did you hear his response on the negative stereotypes?

Ms. FITCH. I heard most of it, Senator.

Senator HATCH. What do you think of those comments made by her attributed to him and his comments back about those comments?

Ms. FITCH. As an historian, I know those comments to be stereotypical.

Senator HATCH. Why would you think she would say that?

Ms. FITCH. Senator, I have no idea. I don't know, but they are certainly kind of pat formulaic statements that people have historically made about black men in this country.

Senator HATCH. Don't they play on white prejudices about black men?

Ms. FITCH. Of course they do, Senator.

◻

Senator HATCH. There is an interesting case that I found called *Carter* v. *Sedgwick County, Kansas*, a 1988 case, dated September 30. It is a Tenth Circuit Court of Appeals case. It is a District Court case. It is a District Court case within the Tenth Circuit.

And do you know which circuit Oklahoma is in?

Judge THOMAS. My guess would be the Tenth Circuit. I remember serving on a moot court panel with a judge from the Tenth Circuit and I believe she was from Tulsa.

Senator HATCH. Well, I have to tell you something, I believe Oklahoma is in the Tenth Circuit, and Utah is also.

An interesting case and I am just going to read one paragraph, if anybody wants to read it. I apologize in advance for some of the language, I really do. It is a civil rights case, interesting civil rights case.

And again I apologize in advance for the language. I just want to read one paragraph. "Plaintiff testified that during the course of her employment she was subjected to numerous racial slurs"—by the way this is an extremely interesting case because the head note says, black female brought suit against county and county officials contending she suffered sexual harassment and was unlawfully terminated from her employment with county on the basis of her race and sex. Now, anybody who wants it, we will make copies for you or you can get it. I will give the citation, as a matter of fact. The citation is 705 F. Supp. 1474, District Court Kansas, 1988.

Let me just read the one paragraph.

Plaintiff testified that during the course of her employment she was subjected to numerous racial slurs and epithets at the hands of the Defendant Brand. And was sexually harassed by Defendant Cameron. Specifically as to Plaintiff's claim of race discrimination. Plaintiff testified that Defendant Brand referred to Plaintiff on several occasions as John's [Cameron] token.

I apologize for this word, but it is in here—"nigger." That is certainly racist.

And at other times, would tell Plaintiff that is was "nigger pick day". Plaintiff claims that Defendant Brand kept a picture of a black family in his office, and when Plaintiff questioned Brand about the picture he boasted of his own.

And the word is used again—"blood and of his sexual conquests of black"—and I am not going to say that word, it is a pejorative term, it is a disgusting term.

So, this man was claiming sexual conquests.

Plaintiff further testified that on one occasion Defendant Brand presented her with a picture of Long Dong Silver— a photo of a black male with an elongated penis.

I apologize again.

Well, it goes on, it gets worse, maybe not worse, but it goes on. That is the public opinion that's available in any law library. I have to tell you I am sure it is available there at the law school in Oklahoma and it is a sexual harassment case.

I am really concerned about this matter. Because, first of all, I really don't believe for one instant, knowing you for 11 years, sitting in on four confirmation processes, having them pick at you, and fight at you, and find fault all the way through—and it is fair game with regard to what you did and what you tried to do, what your excesses were with regard to your job, what your failures were, what your successes were—all of that is fair game and it happened.

And you went through it and you held your dignity and answered all the questions. You were confirmed three times in a row. This is your fourth time. And you should be confirmed here. Never once were you attacked like this by anybody and I know you, and the people who know you the best and that involves hundreds of people, think the world of you. They know you are a good man. They know this woman's a good woman. And this is not consistent with reality. And I am not going to find fault beyond that with Professor Hill. I liked her, too, she presented herself well.

I will tell you the Juan Williams piece in the Washington Post telling how all these interest groups have scratched through everything on earth to try and get something on you, all over the country, all over this town, all over your agency, all over everybody. And there is [sic] a lot of slick lawyers in those groups, slick lawyers, the worst kind. There are some great ones, too, and it may have been a great one who found the reference to "Long Dong Silver", which I find totally offensive.

And I find it highly ironic that you have testified here, today, that used against you by one who taught civil rights, who came from one of the five best law schools in the country, who is an intelligent, apparently decent African-American, used against you, a bunch of black stereotype accusations.

What do you think about that?

Judge THOMAS. Senator, as I have indicated before and I will continue to say this and believe this, I have been harmed. I have been harmed. My family has been harmed. I have been harmed worse than I have ever been harmed in my life. I wasn't harmed by the Klan, I wasn't harmed by the Knights of Camelia, I wasn't harmed by the Aryan race, I wasn't harmed by a racist group, I was harmed by this process, this process which accommodated these attacks on me. If someone wanted to block me from the Supreme Court of the United States because of my views on the Constitution, that is fine. If someone wanted to block me because they felt I was not qualified, that is fine. If someone wanted to block me because they don't like the composition of the Court, that is fine. But to destroy me, Senator, I would have preferred an assassin's bullet to this kind of living hell that they have put me and my family through.

Senator HATCH. Let me just give you one more. Everybody knows that the worst nightmare for any trial lawyer is to have a person who has an impeccable background, a good appearance and appears to believe everything that person is saying, testifying. And it happens in lots of trials, lots of them.

I have been there, believe it or not. I have lost a lot of the skills, but I have been there. Sixteen years here causes you to lose a lot of things. You almost lose your mind sometimes, and some have suggested that I have, from time to time. But I am just going to give you one more because it really offends me, maybe it doesn't anybody else, maybe I am wrong. But I don't think so. I have been through this a lot of times. I have been through this, only usually—Senator Biden, I am really going to have to take more time than a half hour, if you will let me, I have got to finish this and I have got to finish my line of questions.

The CHAIRMAN. Without objection, you can take the time you want and then we will just allocate the time.

Senator HATCH. Thank you. I really appreciate that.

She testified:

> One of the oddest episodes I remember was an occasion in which Thomas was drinking a Coke in his office, he got up from the table, at which we were working, went over to his desk to get the coke, looked at the can and asked, "who has put pubic hair on my coke?"

That's what she said. Did you ever say that?

Judge THOMAS. No, absolutely not.

Senator HATCH. Did you ever think of saying something like that?

Judge THOMAS. No.

Senator HATCH. That's a gross thing to say, isn't it?

Whether it is said by you or by somebody else, it is a gross thing to say, isn't it?

Judge THOMAS. As far as I am concerned, Senator, it is and it is something I did not nor would I say.

Senator HATCH. Ever read this book?

Judge THOMAS. No.

Senator HATCH. The Exorcist?

Judge THOMAS. No, Senator.

Senator HATCH. Ever see the movie?

Judge THOMAS. I have seen only the scene with the bed flapping.

Senator HATCH. I am going to call your attention, and keep in mind, Juan Williams said, this great journalist for the Washington Post, I differ with him, but he is a great journalist. I don't differ with him on everything, we agree on a lot of things.

We certainly agree in this area. But he wrote down what they have tried to do to smear you, he wrote down that they have the whole country blanketed trying to dig up dirt, just like you have said it, just like you have said it. And let me tell you these are not itty-bitty tort attorney investigators. These are the smartest attorneys from the best law schools in the land, all paid for at the public interest expense, that is what is ruining our country, in large measure because some of these groups, not all of them—many of these public interests are great, I don't mean to malign them all—but a number of them are vicious. We saw it in the Bork matter and we are seeing it here.

You said you never did say this, "Who has put pubic hair on my Coke." You never did talk to her about "Long Dong Silver." I submit, those things were found.

On page 70 of this particular version of the Exorcist,

> Oh, Burk, sighed Sharon. In a guarded tone, she described an encounter between the Senator and the director. Dennings had remarked to him, in passing, said Sharon, that there appeared to be an alien pubic hair floating around in my gin.

Do you think that was spoken by happenstance? She would have us believe that you were saying these things, because you wanted to date her? What do you think about that, Judge?

Judge THOMAS. Senator, I think this whole affair is sick.

Senator HATCH. I think it's sick, too.

Judge THOMAS. I don't think I should be here today. I don't think that this inquisition should be going on. I don't think that the FBI file should have been leaked. I don't think that my name should have been destroyed, and I don't think that my family and I should have been put through this ordeal, and I don't think that our country should be brought low by this kind of garbage.

Senator HATCH. These two FBI agents told her to be as specific as she could possibly be, and yet she never said anything about Long Dong Silver or pubic hair to them. She didn't say it in her statement, her four-page statement, which is extensive, single-spaced, four pages. But she said it yesterday.

I don't know whether you noticed, but I noticed that whole entourage—not her family, they looked beautiful, they look like wonderful people to me. Look at her parents, they are clearly good people, clearly, her sisters, clearly good people. But I saw the entourage come in, and I'm not saying they did this, but you can bet your bottom dollar that their are very [sic] possible stereotype, to use your terms—but I never fully understood that—every possible stereotype that could be dug up. . . .

❑

Senator Heflin followed up on the 10th Circuit sexual harassment case and on the passage in the Exorcist, *then inexplicably introduced a new, irrelevant topic into the proceedings—date rape—although no one had made any allegations concerning that issue at all.*

Senator HEFLIN. Judge, Senator Hatch brought up the issue of the Tenth Circuit case pertaining to Long Dong Silver, and in your responsibility as head of the EEOC, do you keep up with cases involving discrimination and sexual harassment that the Circuit Court of Appeals may decide?

Judge THOMAS. Senator, the way that that is normally done is that if there is a significant case, I did not read specific cases, but if there were a significant case the general counsel would summarize that, would analyze it, and if necessary, would simply provide us with a copy of it.

I would not normally read Circuit Court opinions unless it was breaking new ground.

Senator HEFLIN. Well, in the field of employment discrimination, in a year's time how many Circuit Court of Appeals opinions, cases have been written, say, per year, over the last several years?

Judge THOMAS. Senator, I don't know.

Senator HEFLIN. Now, let me ask you, did you read this case of the Tenth Circuit that involved this Long Dong Silver?

Judge THOMAS. Senator, this is the first I have heard of it, and I have not read it.

Senator HEFLIN. The term, Long Dong Silver, whatever else might be given to it, I have been told that there is a movie, a pornographic movie in regards to it. Have you ever heard of the name of that?

Judge THOMAS. No, Senator.

Senator HEFLIN. Now, this issue of pubic hair in the coke, did you read the book, the Exorcist?

Judge THOMAS. No Senator.

Senator HEFLIN. Quite a few people have read it, haven't they, from what I understand. I haven't read it, but—

Judge THOMAS. I don't know. I can't testify. I think the publisher would have to tell you that, Senator.

◻

Senator HEFLIN. . . . You, in your opening statement made a statement about the lack of corroborating witnesses. I had some discussion with two other people and we were talking about how unusual this case was and how it has attracted attention nationally of people because of its unusualness. And one of them remarked it is not unusual that this occurs ann [sic] the type of situation we are in today occurs in almost every date rape case that occurs, that there are no witnesses.

And usually in regard to the prosecution in that case and the defense of those cases, a somewhat wider latitude is allowed relative to background pertaining to it.

Senator HATCH. Mr. Chairman, excuse me, Senator, I have to object to this line of questioning. I don't know of anybody who has accused him of date rape. Is [sic] what you are driving at?

Senator HEFLIN. Well, it is a common term as I understand it date rape is where people go out on dates and rape occurs.

Senator HATCH. What does that have to do with this?

Senator HEFLIN. Well, the analogy between the two is the analogy that in the trial of such cases, that broader leeway is given relative to investigations to tendencies of people that are involved in it in the past. And the only thing I am asking you, Judge, is whether or not you refused to answer any questions other than what may have occurred in employment. Do you continue to do that?

Judge THOMAS. Oh, absolutely, Senator. I will not be further humiliated by this process. I think I have suffered enough, my family has suffered enough. I think that I have attempted to address all of the questions with respect to my relationship with Ms. Hill in the work force and I think enough is enough.

Senator HEFLIN. I had an old trial lawyer tell me one time, Judge, that if you got the facts on your side, argue the facts to the jury. If you got the law on your side, argue the law to the judge. If you have got neither, confuse the issue with other parties.

Senator HATCH. You mean like date rape?

❑

Senator HEFLIN. Mr. Chairman, I will just take 30 seconds. I want to clarify one thing, one member of my staff thought there might be some misunderstanding about it. I accused no one of rape, of date rape at all. And the only thing I was using it as a comparison was that when you have date rape offenses you seldom have any witnesses, any corroborating witnesses and I was using that to the analogy that in this instance we don't have any witnesses or any corroborating witnesses at the fact, that's all.

❑

Senator SPECTER. . . . [I]t was my question to Professor Hill about the USA article on October 9, "Anita Hill was told by Senate staffers her signed affidavit alleging sexual harassment by Clarence Thomas would be the instrument that would quietly, and behind the scenes, would force him to withdraw his name."

Now, I am about to go through the transcript where I asked Professor Hill about this repeatedly and at one point she consulted her attorney and throughout an extensive series of questions yesterday morning flatly denied that any Senate staffer had told her that her coming forward would lead to your withdrawal. And in the afternoon she flatly changed that by identifying a Senate staffer who she finally said told her that she was told that if she came forward you would withdraw or might withdraw your nomination.

The transcript, which is prepared overnight, does not reveal the part where she consulted with her attorney, but I asked my staffers to review the tape, because I recollected that and they did find the spot, which I shall refer to, but I want to make that plain that it is not in the written transcript.

I start, Judge Thomas, at page 79 of the record, where I questioned Professor Hill, that USA Today reported on October 9.

Anita Hill was told by Senate staffers her signed affidavit alleging sexual harassment by Clarence Thomas would be the instrument that, quietly and behind the scenes, would force him to withdraw his name.

I am not reading all of it, because I cannot in the time we have here, but if anybody disagrees with anything I read, they are at liberty to add whatever they choose.

On page 80:

Question: Did anybody ever tell you that, by providing the statement that there would be a move to request Judge

Thomas to withdraw his nomination? Ms. Hill: I don't recall any story about using this to press anyone.

Later, on page 80:

Ms. Hill: I don't recall anything being said about him being pressed to resign.

Page 81:

Senator Specter: Well, aside from 'quietly and behind the scenes pressing him to withdraw,' any suggestion that just the charges themselves in writing would result in Judge Thomas withdrawing and going away? Ms. Hill: I don't recall that at all, no.

Skipping ahead to page 82—this is in the middle of one of my questions:

You have testified with some specificity about what happened 10 years ago. I would ask you to press your recollection as to what happened within the last month. Ms. Hill: And I have done that, Senator, and I don't recall that comment. I do recall there might have been some suggestion that if the FBI did the investigation, that the Senate might get involved, that there may be that a number of things might occur, but I really, I have to be honest with you, I cannot verify the statement that you are asking me to verify. There is not really more that I can tell you on that.

Then skipping ahead to page 84:

Senator Specter: Would you not consider a matter of real importance, if someone said to you, professor, you won't have to go public, your name won't have to be disclosed, you won't have to do anything, just sign the affidavit, and this, as USA Today reports, would be the instrument that, quietly and behind the scenes, would force him to withdraw his name. Now, I am asking you whether it happened. I am asking you now only, if it did happen, whether that would be the kind of a statement to you which would be important and impressed upon you that you could remember in the course of four or five weeks.

Now, it is at this time that she consulted with her attorney, according to my recollection and according to my staff's, looking at the tape. And then she says:

I don't recall a specific statement and I cannot say whether that comment would have stuck in my mind, I really cannot say this.

In the afternoon session, I asked Professor Hill—
Senator [PAUL] SIMON. What page are you referring to?
Senator SPECTER. Page 203—to begin, if you could, and proceed from there to account who called you and what those conversations consisted of as it led to your coming forward to the committee.

Then, on a long answer inserted at the end, which was not responsive, because I wasn't asking about the USA Today article any more, she says—and this appears at the bottom of 203.

It even included something to the effect that the information might be presented to the candidate and to the White House, there was some indication that the candidate—excuse me—the nominee might not wish to continue the process.

Then, on the following page, 204, continuing in the middle of the page:

Senator Specter: So, Mr. Brudney did tell you that Judge Thomas might not wish to continue to go forward with his nomination, if you came forward? Ms. Hill: Yes.

Now, Judge Thomas, what do you make of that change of testimony?

Judge THOMAS. Senator, I think that the individuals such as Jim Brudney, Senator Metzenbaum's staffer on the Education and Labor Committee, should be brought to hearings like this to confront the people in this country for this kind of effort, and I think that they should at some point have to confront my family.

◻

Senator [HOWARD M.] METZENBAUM. Mr. Chairman, there seems to be some issue made as to the conduct of Mr. Brudney, who is the Director of my Labor Subcommittee. Mr. Brudney is as [sic] very honorable and able and dedicated person on my staff.

Mr. Brudney was performing his responsibilities in that connection by inquiring into the background of the nominee to be Associate Justice of the Supreme Court. That came about by reason of the fact that Mr. Brudney and his staff had considerable knowledge concerning Judge Thomas when he was up for confirmation by reason of his activities at the Equal Employment Opportunity Commission.

There is no secret about the fact, on the basis of those conclusions, this Senator decided not to vote for your confirmation to the Circuit Court of Appeals.

But Mr. Brudney was inquiring into what facts were concerning the thoughts of your former employees. He and his staff were doing it. The first call was actually made on September— earlier than September 9. When Mr. Brudney was informed that there were certain allegations concerning the possibility of sexual harassment, he did exactly what any other staffer should have done.

He performed his responsibilities and performed them well. He reported them to me and I told him to immediately turn them over to the Judiciary Committee staff. That is what he did. The fact that Ms. Hill and he had a conversation as to what might develop by reason of her speaking out has already been spoken to in the transcript.

Now, Judge Hill, I have a lot of respect for you—Judge Thomas, excuse me, I apologize—Judge Thomas, I have to say to you that these are important allegations. These are allegations concerning the issue of sexual harassment, and I can only say this to you: Mr. Brudney would have been irresponsible had he not brought the matter to my attention, and I would have been irresponsible if I did not direct him to bring it to the attention of the Judiciary Committee, in order that the Judiciary Committee might investigate the matter. Mr. Brudney did not arrive at any conclusion, I did not arrive at any conclusion, and the subject of this hearing has not, as yet, arrive [sic] at any conclusion, and I doubt very much that it will arrive at any specific conclusion.

But I want to make it clear that Mr. Brudney was doing what he should have done, and had he done less he would have been irresponsible. And had this Senator and this committee done less, it would have been irresponsible.

Sexual harassment is too important an issue to sweep under the rug.

Judge THOMAS. Senator, it was not swept under the rug. This issue was investigated by the FBI and then leaked to the press, and I do not share your view that this was not concocted. This has caused me great pain and my family great pain, and God is my judge, not you, Senator Metzenbaum.

❏

Senator HEFLIN. All right, well, we get back down to the whole issue here is, who is telling the truth, what the motives are? And have you given any other thought, has any other thought come to your mind as to what her motive might be?

Judge THOMAS. Senator, as I said before, I think you should ask the people who helped concoct this and the people who leaked it to the press what the motives were.

❏

The CHAIRMAN. Thank you.

Now, we are down to Senators having five minutes and I will begin to yield back and forth. Judge, let me make sure I understand one thing. Do you believe that interest groups went out and got Professor Hill to make up a story or do you believe Professor Hill had a story, untrue from your perspective that, as referred to here, that groups went out and found. Which do you believe?

Judge THOMAS. Senator, I believe that someone, some interest group, I don't care who it is, in combination came up with this story and used this process to destroy me.

The CHAIRMAN. Got Professor Hill to say, to make up a story?

Judge THOMAS. I believe that in combination this story was developed or concocted to destroy me.

The CHAIRMAN. With Professor Hill? I mean it is a critical question. Are you saying with Professor Hill that a group went out—

Judge THOMAS. That's just my view, Senator.

The CHAIRMAN. I know, I am trying to make sure I understand it.

Judge THOMAS. There are no details to it or anything else. The story developed. I do not believe—the story is not true. The allegations are false and my view is that others put it together and developed this.

The CHAIRMAN. And put it in Professor Hill's mouth?

Judge THOMAS. I don't know. I don't know how it got there. All I know is the story is here and I think it was concocted.

The CHAIRMAN. Well, Judge, I know you believe that and I am not here to be able to or attempt to, at this moment, refute that. There has been an assertion that has just been made and I want to know whether you would agree with it, that—it is important for us to keep our eye on the ball here—either Professor Hill had a story that she told someone and it was taken advantage of by being leaked. That is one thing. She says that. And the other story that seems to be being painted now, not by you, I am asking what you believe, is that a group sat down, decided to make up a story and found a willing vessel in Professor Hill and got her to say it.

Now, they are fundamentally different things in terms of culpability.

Judge THOMAS. Senator, those distinctions are irrelevant to me. The story is false. And the story is here and the story was developed to harm me.

The CHAIRMAN. Thank you.

Judge THOMAS. And it did harm me.

❑

Senator HATCH. . . . Judge, when the President asked you at Kennebunkport whether you and your family could take what would follow in the process, did you have any idea whether you were going to have to "take"? Could you have guessed that some people, including people on this committee, people in the media and others would dredge up stories about drug use, wife-beating, advocating Louis Farahkan's [sic] anti-semitism [sic], lying about your neutrality in Roe v. Wade, sexual harassment, maybe even implications of other things? Did you think you would have to face scurrilous accusations like those, which you have refuted?

Judge THOMAS. Senator, I expected it to be bad and I expected awful treatment throughout the process, I expected to be a sitting duck for the interest groups, I expected them to attempt to kill me, and, yes, I even expected personally attempts on my life. That is just how much I expected.

I did not expect this circus. I did not expect this charge against my name. I expected people to do anything, but not this. And if by going through this, another nominee in the future or another American won't have to go through it, then sobeit, but I did not expect this treatment and I did not expect to lose my name, my reputation, my integrity to do public service. Again, I did not ask to be nominated, I did not lobby for it, I did not beg for it, I did not aspire to it.

I was perfectly happy on the U.S. Court of Appeals for the D.C. Circuit, which is a lifetime appointment. I did not expect to lose my life in the process.

Senator HATCH. A Washington Post article just today said that you said—and I recall you saying—you told of reporters sneaking into my garage, interest group lobbyists swarming over divorce papers looking for dirt. I remember you said this is not the American dream, this is Kafka-esque, it has got to stop, enough is enough.

The Post article goes on to say some activists were unmoved by Thomas' emotional plea, dismissing it as a last-ditch effort to salvage his nomination. "The major groups don't have anything to apologize for," said one of the civil rights activists. He went on to say, "The battle has been fought on policy and philosophy," although he acknowledged "it has taken a distressing turn."

"That turn," the article goes on to say, "illustrates the increasingly symbiotic relationship between committee staffers, liberal interest groups and the news media. It is a phenomena [sic] that accelerated with the Reagan administration's attempts to insure conservative domination of the judiciary in the 1980's.

Many thought it reached its ultimate expression in the battle over the nomination of Robert H. Bork to the Supreme Court in 1987. But within days after President Bush announced Thomas' nomination, liberal activist groups began the search for ammunition they hoped could defeat him. An informal coalition that included Cropp"—I suppose he is with people for the American Way—"Kate Michelman of the National Abortion Rights Action League, Nan Aaron of the Alliance for Justice, and others began holding almost daily strategy sessions, at first restricting their probes to exposing what they viewed as his track record as a rigid Reagan administration ideologue. Cropp said that his organization, which had played a pivotal role in the Bork fight"—I might add that they put ads in the paper and I accused them of 99, as I recall, errors in the ad, and they never answered the accusations, they could not, really.

"Cropp said that his organization, which had played a pivotal role in the Bork fight, assigned four full-time staffers, several interns and four other field organizers to anti-Thomas activities. The group also filed Freedom of Information requests for copies and videotapes of all his public speeches and videotapes while he headed the Equal Employment Opportunity Commission and the Office of Civil Rights in the Department of Education."

Naturally, they can do that if they want to, but these are only a few groups that are mentioned, and there are literally hundreds, if not thousands of groups in this area, and the groups, many feel, have taken over the process.

And in the process the ideology becomes more important than truth, it becomes more important than integrity, it becomes more important than ethics, it becomes more important than preserving people's reputations, it becomes more important than simple, basic decency to human beings.

I think it was said best, again I cite Juan Williams' statement, he said, "This desperate search for ammunition to shoot down Thomas has turned the 102 days since President Bush nominated him for a seat on the Supreme Court into a liberal's nightmare." Now, this is a journalist who is not particularly conservative, but nevertheless a great journalist.

"Here is indiscriminate"—didn't quite mean it the way that some have taken it, he is a great journalist and I mean that. I don't know how people take that implication but I mean that.

Senator [STROM] THURMOND. Tell them the name.

Senator HATCH. Juan Williams. "Here is indiscriminate"— he is describing, he is describing this desperate search for ammunition—"Here is indiscriminate mean-spirited mud slinging supported by the so-called champions of fairness. Liberal politicians, unions, civil rights groups, and women's organizations, they have been mindlessly led into mob action against one man by the Leadership Conference on Civil Rights. Moderate and liberal Senators operating in the proud tradition of men, such as Hubert Humphrey and Robert Kennedy, have allowed themselves to become sponsors of smear tactics that have historically been associated with the gutter politics of a Lee Atwater or crazed right-wing self-promoters like Senator Joseph McCarthy. During the hearings on his nomination, Thomas was subjected to a glaring double-standard."

Now, for those of you who laugh, why is it that Juan Williams is one of the few who has pointed out this glaring double-standard. Laugh at that, laugh at that. That's what I am talking about here. I am not talking about liberal and conservative politics. I am talking about decency. I am talking about our country, America.

Thomas was subjected to a glaring double-standard. I have never seen it worse, never. When he did not answer questions that former nominees David Souter and Anthony Kennedy did not answer he was pilloried for his evasiveness. One opponent testified that her basis for opposing him was his lack of judicial experience. She did not know that Supreme Court Justices, such as liberal icons Earl Warren, and Felix Frankfurter, as well as current Chief Justice William Rehnquist had no judicial experience before taking a seat on the high court.

There is a lot more that could be said. But he says a very interesting paragraph and I think it does sum it up, he said, "This slimy exercise orchestrated in the form of leaks of an affidavit to the Leadership Conference on Civil Rights is an abuse of the Senate confirmation process, an abuse of Senate rules, and an unforgivable abuse of a human being named Clarence Thomas."

❏

Dr. Fitch in later testimony discussed with Senator Grassley the issue of blacks who differed with the established black leadership.

Senator GRASSLEY. . . . I had a black leader in my State advise to be against him and this was the words [sic] of this black leader, "He doesn't even speak our language."

What is meant by that? I honestly don't know.

Ms. FITCH. Senator, I don't know what the person who said that meant, but I think it means that that person is somehow perceived to be outside the group, is not in some perceived lock-step. And I think if you look at the history of black people in this country you see that people have always had diverse views. We are not a monolithic community in thought. And I think that is a huge mistake for the dominant society to think and for us to buy into.

And I suppose that—I don't know the situation you are talking about—but that is probably what that meant.

Senator GRASSLEY. Well, have you ever heard other black American leaders use the expression, he doesn't even speak our language?

Ms. FITCH. I don't know if I have heard the exact words, but I have gotten the distinct impression from working and watching

Judge Thomas and how he seems to be perceived by black leaders, some of them, that that is something that they are saying, in effect, if they are not using those exact words. So I understand what that means.

Senator GRASSLEY. Well, it is almost like denouncing the individuality that we worship in America.

Ms. FITCH. I think, Senator, the problem is that when you are a community under siege it is very difficult for people to want to allow diversity of opinion. It is understandable. I don't like it but it is understandable and I don't think in any situation where you have communities that are considered minority and where there are a majority community around them that you are going to find this kind of attitude.

Senator GRASSLEY. In other words, we are all going to hang together or hang separately?

Ms. FITCH. That, I think that is one way of explaining it, yes, Senator. That may be a simplistic way of doing it. I am sure there are other things involved, but, certainly that is one way of putting it. And I don't think it is just true in this country, it's probably true in South Africa, and in other places where there are communities under seige within the countries that they live in, and the societies that they live in.

Senator GRASSLEY. So you intellectually lynch the people who do want to—

Ms. FITCH. That's one way of doing it, Senator. That is probably the lesser of many evils.

❑

Senator HATCH. . . . I would like you to describe now, for this gathering, what it is like to be accused of sexual harassment. Tell us what it feels like. And let me add the word, unjustly accused of sexual harassment.

Judge THOMAS. Senator, as I have said throughout these hearings, the last two and a half weeks have been a living hell. I think I have died a thousand deaths. What it means is living on one hour a night's sleep. It means losing 15 pounds in two weeks. It means being unable to eat, unable to drink, unable to think about anything but this and wondering why and how? It means wanting to give up. It means losing the belief in our system, and in this system, and in this process. Losing a belief in a sense of fairness and honesty and decency. That is what it has meant to me.

When I appeared before this committee for my real confirmation hearing, it was hard. I would have preferred it to be better. I would have preferred for more members to vote for me. But I had a faith that, at least this system was working in some fashion, though imperfectly.

I don't think this is right. I think it's wrong. I think it's wrong for the country. I think it's hurt me and I think it's hurt the country. I have never been accused of sex harassment. And anybody who knows me knows I am adamantly opposed to that, adamant, and yet, I sit here accused. I will never be able to get my name back, I know it.

The day I get to receive a phone call on Saturday night, last Saturday night, about 7:30 and told that this was going to be in the press, I died. The person you knew, whether you voted for me or against me, died.

In my view, that is an injustice.

Senator HATCH. Now, Judge—

Judge THOMAS. As I indicated earlier, it is an injustice to me, but it is a bigger injustice to this country. I don't think any American, whether that person is homeless, whether that person earns a minimum wage or is unemployed, whether that person runs a corporation or small business, black, white, male, female should have to go through this for any reason.

The person who appeared here for the real confirmation hearings believed that it was OK to be nominated to the Supreme Court and have a tough confirmation hearing. This person, if asked by George Bush today, would he want to be nominated would refuse flatly, and would advise any friend of his to refuse, it is just not worth it.

Senator HATCH. Judge, you are here though. Some people have been spreading the rumor that perhaps you are going to withdraw. What is Clarence Thomas going to do? What is Clarence Thomas going to do?

Judge THOMAS. I would rather die than withdraw. If they are going to kill me, they are going to kill me.

Senator HATCH. So you would still like to serve on the Supreme Court?

Judge THOMAS. I would rather die than withdraw from the process. Not for the purpose of serving on the Supreme Court but for the purpose of not being driven out of this process. I will not be scared. I don't like bullies. I have never run from bullies. I never cry uncle and I am not going to cry uncle today whether I want to be on the Supreme Court or not.

❑

Senator GRASSLEY. You haven't mentioned your grandfather at all this particular sitting. I would like to have you tell me what you think, advice he would give to you if he were advising you today.

Judge THOMAS. Well, Senator, in 1983—and this is something that I said during my real confirmation hearings—when I was getting hammered in the public and getting criticized, and I complained to him, he told me to stand up for what I believe in. That is what he would tell me today: not to quit, not to turn tail, not to cry "uncle," and not to give up until I am dead. He had another statement: "Give out but don't give up." That is what he would say to me.

❑

Justice Thomas further elaborated on his views of the confir-mation process.

Judge THOMAS. This process is wrong, Senator. There is no way, as far as I am concerned, that you can validate it.

Senator KOHL. I don't want to—

Judge THOMAS. The allegations, anyone can make an allega-tion. I deny those allegations. I have always cooperated with the FBI. Think about who you are talking to. I have been a public figure for 10 years. I have been confirmed four times. I have had five FBI background checks. I have had stories written about me, I have had groups that despise me, looking into my back-ground.

I have had people who wanted to do me great harm. You are talking about a person who ran an agency—two agencies to fight discrimination, who, if I did anything stupid like this, gross like this, had everything to lose, who adamantly preached against it. It just seems as though I am here to prove the negative in a forum without rules and after the fact.

I think that all this has done is give a forum to people who can make terrible charges against individuals who have to come here for confirmation. I think this is all this has done and it has harmed me greatly, Senator.

That is not to say that sex harassment is not serious. My record speaks for itself on that. But there is a forum for that. You have agencies for that. You have courts for that to deal with those. You cannot deal with those in this process in this manner.

What you are doing is you are inviting and validating people making very serious charges against other individuals who do not have the capacity to extricate themselves from it.

❑

Judge THOMAS. Senator, there is also a positive side of this.

Senator DECONCINI. Tell me what it is, except raising the

awareness of sex harassment, and I don't say that is minimal, but I think that awareness is out there and has been out there for a long time, if I may say myself, and I didn't need this experience to raise it for me, but please don't let me interrupt what you say is the positive side. Believe me, I am looking for one; I am praying for one.

Judge THOMAS. During this process, the last 105 days, and the last two and a half weeks especially, I have never had such an outpouring of love and affection and friendship in people who know me, not people making these scurrilous assertions but people who know me, supporting me and caring for me, helping me to recover from it and survive it—my wife; my son, whose reaction is just to be terribly angry.

I think it showed me just how vulnerable I am as a human being, and any American, that these kinds of charges can be given validity in a process such as this, and the destruction it can do. It has given me that sense.

I think it has also shown people in our country what is happening. I didn't want them to see what happened to me. I didn't want my personal life or allegations about my sexual habits or anything else broadcast in every living room in the United States. But they see this process for what it is, and I think that is good, and hopefully it never happens to another American.

Yes, I can heal. As I said in my opening remarks, I will simply walk down the Hill, if I am not confirmed, that will be it, and continue my job as Court of Appeals Judge, and hopefully live a long life, enjoy my neighbors and my friends, my son, cut my grass, go to McDonald's, and drive my car, and just be a good citizen and a good judge and a good father and a good husband. Yes, I will survive. My question was, will the country survive, and hopefully it will.

Senator DeCONCINI. And if you are confirmed?

Judge THOMAS. I will survive, a different person. I would have hoped, Senator, when I was nominated, that it would have been an occasion for joy. There has never been a single day of joy in this process. There has never been one minute of joy in having been nominated to the Supreme Court of the United States of America.

Senator DeConcini. Judge Thomas, you said—correct me if I am wrong—after 10 days or whatever it was, 90 witnesses and your 5 days, I thought you were not just being gracious but being sincere, where you thanked the chairman and this committee and, as you said today, you would have liked to receive more votes here but you didn't, and that was the process. As I remember your words, you said, "I think I have been treated fairly, and I have no quarrel or no ill feelings." Am I restating that correct [sic], how you felt after your formal hearing?

Judge THOMAS. That is right, Senator.

Senator DeConcini. And I can understand that you don't feel that way today, and my question continues to go to the sense of you being confirmed. What does it do to somebody? Does it affect their ability to approach cases, as you indicated, and satisfactorily so to this Senator, approach cases as a Supreme Court Judge? Can you be reborn in the sense of the loss that you have had to suffer here in the last two weeks? And how do you cope with it, if you care to say? And if you don't, I will understand.

Judge THOMAS. Senator, there is one thing that I have learned over my life, and that is that I will be back.

The other thing that I have learned in this process are things that we discussed in the real confirmation hearing, and that is our rights being protected, what rights we have as citizens of this country, what constitutional rights, what is our relationship with our government. And as I sit here on matters such as privacy, matters such as procedures for charges against individuals in a criminal context or a civil context, this has heightened my awareness of the importance of those protections, the importance of some thing that we discussed in theory—privacy, due process, equal protection fairness.

Senator DeConcini. Judge, is it safe to say that—what a way to have to come to it, and this Senator was satisfied you didn't have to come to it, that you met the threshold for my vote—what you are now saying to us is that through this God-awful experience you will be more sensitive towards the rights of the accused, and that that is because your rights have been violated. Is that correct?

Judge Thomas. I have been an accused.

Senator DeConcini. And your rights—

Judge Thomas. Were violated, as far as—

Senator DeConcini. —were violated?

Judge Thomas. I think strongly so.

Senator DeConcini. Thank you, Judge Thomas.

❑

T̲estimony of a panel consisting of J.C. Alvarez, River North Distributing, Chicago, IL; Nancy E. Fitch, Philadelphia, PA; Diane Holt, Management Analyst, Office of the Chairman, Equal Employment Opportunity Commission, Washington, DC.; and Phyllis Berry Myers, Alexandria, VA

❏

TESTIMONY OF J.C. ALVAREZ

Ms. ALVAREZ. My name is J.C. Alvarez. I am a business-woman from Chicago. I am a single mom, raising a 15-year-old son, running a business. In many ways, I am just a John Q. Public from Middle America, not unlike a lot of the people watching out there and not unlike a lot of your constituents.

But the political world is not a world that I am unfamiliar with. I spent nine years in Washington, DC. A year with Senator Danforth, two years with the Secretary of Education, a short stint at the Federal Emergency Management Agency, and four years as Special Assistant to Clarence Thomas at the EEOC.

Because of this past political experience, I was just before this Committee a couple of weeks ago speaking in support of Clarence Thomas's nomination to the Supreme Court. I was then and I still am in favor of Clarence Thomas being on the Supreme Court.

When I was asked to testify the last time, I flew to Washington, D.C., very proud and happy to be part of the process of nominating a Supreme Court Justice. When I was sitting here before you last time, I remember why I had liked working in Washington, DC., so much—the intellectual part of it, the high quality of the debate. Although I have to admit when I had to listen to some of your questioning and postulating and politick-

95

ing, I remembered why I had left. And I thought at that point that certainly I had seen it all.

After the hearings, I flew back to Chicago, back to being John Q. Public, having a life very far removed from this political world, and it would have been easy to stay away from politics in Washington, DC. Like most of your constituents out there, I have more than my share of day-to-day challenges that have nothing to do with Washington, DC., and politics. As I said before, I am a single mom, raising a teenager in today's society, running a business, making ends meet—you know, soccer games, homework, doing laundry, paying bills, that is my day-to-day reality.

Since I left Washington, DC., I vote once every four years for President and more frequently for other State and local officials. And I could have remained outside of the political world for a long, long time and not missed it. I don't need this. I needed to come here like I needed a hole in the head. It cost me almost $900 just for the plane ticket to come here, and then there is the hotel and other expenses. And I can assure you that especially in these recessionary times I have got lots of other uses for that money.

So why did I come? Why didn't I just stay uninvolved and apolitical? Because, Senators, like most real Americans who witness a crime being committed, who witness an injustice being done, I could not look the other way and pretend that I did not see it. I had to get involved.

In my real life, I have walked down the street and seen a man beating up a woman and I have stepped in and tried to stop it. I have walked through a park and seen a group of teenage hoodlums taunting an old drunk man and I have jumped in the middle of it. I don't consider myself a hero. No, I am just a real American from Middle America who will not stand by and watch a crime being committed and walk away. To do so would be the beginning of the deterioration of society and of this great country.

CONFRONTING THE FUTURE • 97

No, Senators, I cannot stand by and watch a group of thugs beat up and rob a man of his money any more than I could have stayed in Chicago and stood by and watched you beat up an innocent man and rob him blind. Not of his money. That would have been too easy. You could pay that back. No, you have robbed a man of his name, his character and his reputation.

And what is amazing to me is that you didn't do it in a dark alley and you didn't do it in the dark of night. You did it in broad daylight, in front of all America, on television, for the whole world to see. Yes, Senators, I am witnessing a crime in progress and I cannot just look the other way. Because I am John Q. Public and I am getting involved.

I know Clarence Thomas and I know Anita Hill. I was there from the first few weeks of Clarence coming to the Commission. I had the office next to Anita's. We all worked together in setting and executing the goals and the direction that the Chairman had for the EEOC. I remember Chris Roggerson, Carlton Stewart, Nancy Fitch, Barbara Parris, Phyllis Berry, Bill Ng, Allyson Duncan, Diane Holt—each of us with our own area of expertise and responsibility, but together all of us a part of Clarence Thomas's hand-picked staff.

I don't know how else to say it, but I have to tell you that it just blew my mind to see Anita Hill testifying on Friday. Honest to goodness, it was like schizophrenia. That was not the Anita Hill that I knew and worked with at EEOC. On Friday, she played the role of a meek, innocent, shy Baptist girl from the South who was a victim of this big, bad man.

I don't know who she was trying to kid. Because the Anita Hill that I knew and worked with was nothing like that. She was a very hard, tough woman. She was opinionated. She was arrogant. She was a relentless debater. And she was the kind of woman who always made you feel like she was not going to be messed with, like she was not going to take anything from anyone.

She was aloof. She always acted as if she was a little bit superior to everyone, a little "holier than thou." I can recall at the time that she had a view of herself and her abilities that did not seem to be based in reality. For example, it was sort of common knowledge around the office that she thought she should have been Clarence's chief legal advisor and that she should have received better assignments.

And I distinctly remember when I would hear about her feeling that way or when I would see her pout in office meetings about assignments that she had gotten, I used to think to myself, "Come on, Anita, let's come down to earth and live in reality." She had only been out of law school a couple of years and her experience and her ability couldn't begin to compare with some of the others on the staff.

But I also have to say that I was not totally surprised at her wanting these assignments because she definitely came across as someone who was ambitious and watched out for her own advancement. She wasn't really a team player, but more someone who looked out for herself first. You could see the same thing in her relationships with others at the office.

☐

You could see that Anita Hill was not a real team player, but more someone who looked out for herself. You could see this even in her relationships with others at the office. She mostly kept to herself, although she would occasionally participate in some of the girl-talk among the women at the office, and I have to add that I don't recall her being particularly shy or innocent about that either.

You see, Senators, that was the Anita Hill that we all knew and we worked with. And that is why hearing her on Friday was so shocking. No, not shocking. It was so sickening. Trust me, the Anita Hill I knew and worked with was a totally different personality from the Anita Hill I heard on Friday. The Anita Hill I knew before was nobody's victim.

The Clarence Thomas I knew and worked with was also not who Anita Hill alleges. Everyone who knows Clarence, knows that he is a very proud and dignified man. With his immediate staff, he was very warm and friendly, sort of like a friend or a father. You could talk with him about your problems, go to him for advice, but, like a father, he commanded and he demanded respect. He demanded professionalism and performance, and he was very strict about that.

Because we were friends outside of the office or perhaps in private, I might have called him Clarence, but in the office he was Mr. CHAIRMAN. You didn't joke around with him, you didn't lose your respect for him, you didn't become too familiar with him, because he would definitely let you know that you had crossed the line.

Clarence was meticulous about being sure that he retained a very serious and professional atmosphere within his office, without the slightest hint of impropriety, and everyone knew it.

We weren't a coffee-klatching group. We didn't have office parties or Christmas parties, because Clarence didn't think it was appropriate for us to give others the impression that we were not serious or professional or perhaps working as hard as everyone else. He wanted to maintain a dignity about his office and his every behavior and action confirmed that.

As his professional colleague, I traveled with him, had lunch and dinner with him, worked with him, one-on-one and with others. Never did he ever lose his respect for me, and never did we ever have a discussion of the type that Ms. Hill alleges. Never was he the slightest bit improper in his behavior with me. In every situation I have shared with Clarence Thomas, he has been the ultimate professional and he has required it of those around him, in particular, his personal staff.

From the moment they surfaced, I thought long and hard

about these allegations. You see, I, too, have experienced sexual harassment in the past. I have been physically accosted by a man in an elevator who I rebuffed. I was trapped in a xerox room by a man who I refused to date. Obviously it is an issue I have experienced, I understand, and I take very seriously.

But having lived through it myself, I find Anita Hill's behavior inconsistent with these charges. I can assure you that when I come into town, the last thing I want to do is call either of these two men up and say hello or see if they want to get together.

To be honest with you, I can hardly remember their names, but I can assure you that I would never try and even maintain a cordial relationship with either one of them. Women who have really been harassed would agree, if he [sic] allegations were true, you put as much distance as you can between yourself and that other person.

What's more, you don't follow them to the next job— especially, if you are a black female, Yale law school graduate. Let's face it, out in the corporate sector, companies are fighting for women with those kinds of credentials. Her behavior just isn't consistent with the behavior of a woman who has been harassed, and it just doesn't make sense.

Senators, I don't know what else to say to have you understand the crime that has been committed here. It has to make all of us suspicious of her motives, when someone of her legal background comes in here at the 11th hour, after 10 years, and having had four other opportunities through congressional hearings to oppose this man, and alleges such preposterous things.

I have been contacted by I think every reporter in the country, looking for dirt. And when I present the facts as I experienced them, it is interesting, they don't print it. It's just not as juicy as her amazing allegations.

What is this country coming to, when an innocent man can be ambushed like this, jumped by a gang whose ring leader is one of his own proteges, Anita Hill? Like Julius Caesar, he must want to turn to her and say, "Et tu, Brutus? You too, Anita?"

As a mother with a child, I can only begin to imagine how Clarence must feel, being betrayed by one of his own. Nothing would hurt me more. And I guess he described it best in his opening statement on Friday. His words and his emotions are still ringing in all of our ears and all of our hearts.

I have done the best I could, Senators, to be honest in my statement to you. I have presented the situation as it was then, as I lived it, side by side, with Clarence and with Anita.

You know, I talked with my mom before I came here, and she reminded me that I was always raised to stand up for what I believed. I have seen an innocent man being mugged in broad daylight, and I have not looked the other way. This John Q. Public came here and got involved.

Senator [EDWARD M.] KENNEDY. [Presiding.] Ms. Fitch?

❑

TESTIMONY OF NANCY E. FITCH

Ms. FITCH. Mr. Chairman, Senator Thurmond, members of the committee: My name is Dr. Nancy Elizabeth Fitch. I have a BA in English literature and political science from Oakland University, which was part of Michigan State University at the time—

Senator THURMOND. Would you please call [sic] the microphone closer to you, so that the people in the back can hear you.

Ms. FITCH. —and a masters and Ph.D. in history from the University of Michigan in Ann Arbor. I have taught at Sangamon State University in Illinois, was a social science research analyst for the Congressional Research Service of the Library of Congress, been a special assistant and historian to the then

Chairman of the U.S. Equal Employment Opportunity Commission, Clarence Thomas, an assistant professor of history at Lynchburg College in Virginia, and presently assistant professor of Africa-American Studies at Temple University, in Philadelphia.

From 1982 to 1989, I worked as a special assistant historian to then Chairman Clarence Thomas of the U.S. Equal Employment Opportunity Commission. I worked for and with him seven years and have known him for nine. I researched the history of African-Americans, people of color and women an [sic] their relationship to issues, including employment, education and training. These were used for background on speeches, special emphasis programming at the Commission and for policy position papers.

I reported only to Judge Thomas, and my responsibilities also included outreach efforts to local colleges and universities and to the DC public schools. Judge Thomas was interested in his staff and himself being mentors and role models, especially, but not only to young people of color.

In these nine years, I have known Clarence Thomas to be a person of great integrity, morally upstanding, professional, a decent person, an exemplary boss. Those years spent in his employ as a Schedule C employee, a political appointee, were the most rewarding of my work life to that time. My returning to higher education I attribute to his persuading me to return to what I loved, not continuing as a bureaucrat, but returning to teaching.

I would like to say Judge Thomas, besides being a person of great moral character, I found to be a most intelligent man. Senator Biden was correct yesterday, when he indicated that the Republican side of the panel might have overlooked its easiest defense, that of dealing with the judge's intelligence.

If these allegations, which I believe to be completely unfounded and vigorously believe unfounded, were true, we would be dealing not only with venality, but with abject stupidity with a person shooting himself in the foot, having given someone else the gun to use at any time.

There is no way Clarence Thomas—CT—would callously venally hurt someone. A smart man, concerned about making a contribution to this country as a public official, recognizing the gravity and weightiness of his responsibilities and public trust, a role model and mentor who would, by his life and work, show the possibilities in America for all citizens given opportunity, well, would a person such as this, Judge Clarence Thomas would never ever make a parallel career in harassment, ask that it not be revealed and expect to have and keep his real career. And I know he did no such thing.

He is a dignified, reserve [sic], deliberative, conscientious man of great conscience, and I am proud to be at his defense.

As I told the FBI agent who interviewed me on Tuesday, October 1st, I trust Judge Thomas completely, he has all of my support and caring earned by nine years of the most positive and affirmative interacting, not only with me, but with other staff and former staff, men and women, and I know he will get back his good name.

Thank you.

Senator KENNEDY. Thank you very much.

Ms. Holt?

❏

TESTIMONY OF DIANE HOLT

Ms. HOLT. Mr. Chairman, Senator Thurmond, and members of this committee: My name is Diane Holt. I am a management analyst in the Office of the Chairman of the Equal Employment Opportunity Commission.

I have known Clarence Thomas for over ten years. For six of those years I worked very closely with him, cheek to cheek, shoulder to shoulder, as his personal secretary. My acquaintance with Judge Thomas began in May of 1981, after he had been appointed as Assistant Secretary for Civil Rights at the Department of Education.

I had been the personal secretary to the outgoing Assistant Secretary for several years. Upon Judge Thomas' arrival at the department, he held a meeting with me, in which he indicated that he was not committed to bringing a secretary with him, and had no wish to displace me. Because he was not familiar with my qualifications, he made no guarantees, but gave me an opportunity to prove myself.

That is the kind of man he is.

In May of 1982, Judge Thomas asked me to go to the EEOC with him, where I worked as his secretary until September of 1987.

I met Professor Hill in the summer of 1981, when she came to work at the Department of Education as attorney advisor to Judge Thomas.

After about a year, Judge Thomas was nominated to be Chairman of the EEOC. He asked both Professor Hill and myself to transfer with him.

Both Ms. Hill and I were excited about the prospect of transferring to the EEOC. We even discussed the greater potential for individual growth at this larger agency. We discussed and expressed excitement that we would be at the right hand of the individual who would run this agency.

When we arrived at the EEOC, because we knew no one else there, Professor Hill and I quickly developed a professional relationship, a professional friendship, often having lunch together.

At no time did Professor Hill intimate, not even in the most subtle of ways, that Judge Thomas was asking her out or subjecting her to the crude, abusive conversations that have been described. Nor did I ever discern any discomfort, when Professor Hill was in Judge Thomas' presence.

Additionally, I never heard anyone at any time make any

reference to any inappropriate conduct in relation to Clarence Thomas.

The Clarence Thomas that I know has always been a motivator of staff, always encouraging others to grow professionally. I personally have benefited from that encouragement and that motivation.

In sum, the Chairman Thomas that I have known for ten years is absolutely incapable of the abuses described by Professor Hill.

Senator KENNEDY. Thank you very much.

Ms. Berry-Myers?

❑

TESTIMONY OF PHYLLIS BERRY-MYERS

Ms. BERRY. You can call me Phyllis Berry, since that was my name that I used throughout my professional life, and that's probably what most people are going to refer to me as.

Mr. Chairman, Senator Thurmond and members of the committee, I am Phyllis Berry.

I know and have worked with both Clarence Thomas and Anita Hill. I have known Judge Thomas since 1979, and Anita Hill since 1982. Once Clarence Thomas was confirmed as the Chairman of the Equal Employment Opportunity Commission and had assumed his duties there, he asked me to come and work with him at the Commission.

I joined him [sic] staff as a special assistant in June of 1982. At the Commission, Chairman Thomas asked that I assume responsibility for three areas: I was to, one, assist in assessing reorganizing his personal staff, scheduling, speech writing, and those kinds of things; two, to assist in professionalizing the Office of Congressional Affairs, as that office was called then;

and, three, assist in reorganizing the Office of Public Affairs, as that office was called then.

Anita Hill was already a member of Clarence Thomas' staff when I joined the Commission.

There are several points to be made:

One: Many of the areas of responsibilities that I had been asked to oversee were areas that Anita Hill handled, particularly congressional affairs and public relations. We, therefore, had to work together. Chris Roggerson was the Director of Congressional Affairs at that time, and Anita Hill worked more under his supervision than Clarence Thomas'.

Two: Clarence Thomas' behavior toward Anita Hill was no more, no less than his behavior towards the rest of his staff. He was respectful, demand [sic] of excellence in our work, cordial, professional, interested in our lives and our career ambitions.

Three: Anita Hill indicated to me that she had been a primary advisor to Clarence Thomas at the Department of Education. However, she seemed to be having a difficult time on his EEOC staff, of being considered as one of many, especially on a staff where others were as equally or more talented than she.

Four: Anita Hill often acted as though she had a right to immediate direct access to the CHAIRMAN. Such access was not always immediately available. I felt she was particularly distressed, when Allyson Duncan became chief of staff and her direct access to the Chairman was even more limited.

Five: I cannot remember anyone, except perhaps Diane Holt, who was regarded as personally close to Anita. She was considered by most of us as somewhat aloof.

In addition, I would like to make these comments:

In her press conference on October 7, 1991, Anita Hill indicated that she did not know me and I did not know her. However, in her testimony before this committee, she affirmed that not only did we know one another, but that we enjoyed a friendly, professional relationship.

Also, she testified that I had the opportunity to observe and did observe her interaction with Clarence Thomas at the office.

Two: [sic] I served at the Department of Education at the same time that Anita Hill and Clarence Thomas were there. One aspect of my job was to assist with the placement of personnel at the department, particularly Schedule C and other Excepted Service appointments, such as Schedule A appointments.

Excepted Service means those positions in Federal Civil Service excepted from the normal, competitive requirements that are authorized by law, Executive Order or regulation.

The Schedule C hiring authority is the means by which political appointees are hired. The Schedule A hiring authority is the means by which attorneys, teachers in overseas dependent school systems, drug enforcement agents in undercover work, et cetera, are hired.

The office that I worked in was also responsible for reviewing any hiring that the department's political appointees made under the excepted service hiring authority. Therefore, in that capacity, I was aware of any excepted service hiring decisions made in the Office of Civil Rights, and that is the office that Clarence Thomas headed at that time, and Anita Hill was hired in that office as a Schedule A employee.

Federal personnel processing procedures require a lot of specific knowledge and a lot of paperwork, and I do not profess to be a Federal personnel expert. But I can attest to the procedures required by our office and the Office of Personnel at the Department of Education at that time.

At the end of such procedures, a new employee would have no doubt whatsoever regarding their status, their grade, their pay, their benefits, their promotion rights, employment rights and obligation as a Federal employee and as an employee in the department.

A new employee would know whether their employment is

classified as permanent or temporary, protected or non-protected, and those kinds of things. Each new employee must sign a form that contains such information, before employment can begin.

The Personnel Department at the Department of Education is a fine one, and it takes pride in thoroughly counseling new employees.

T estimony of a panel consisting of Stanley Grayson, Vice President, Goldman Sachs Law Firm, New York, NY; Carlton Stewart, Stewart Law Firm, Atlanta, GA; John N. Doggett III, Management Consultant, Austin, Texas; and Charles Kothe, former Dean, Oral Roberts University Law School

❑

TESTIMONY OF CHARLES KOTHE

Mr. KOTHE. Mr. Chairman and Senators, my name is Charles A. Kothe. I am of counsel to the firm of Clay, Walker—

Senator THURMOND. If you don't mind, I would get close to the microphone so we can hear you all over the room.

Mr. KOTHE. I am presently of counsel to the firm of Clay, Walker, Jackman, Dempson and Moller in Tulsa, Oklahoma.

During March of 1983 I was acting as the founding dean of the O.W. Coburn School of Law at Oral Roberts University. Being interested in our public relations and in our identity with the American Bar Association Accrediting Committee, I decided to have a program on civil rights. I had conducted many of them over the years.

I contacted the Equal Employment Opportunity Commission and talked to Clarence Thomas. I did not know him before that. He said he would come out to a seminar, and asked if he could bring a member of his staff, and I said of course. And so in April of 1983 we had a seminar on civil rights on our campus, and that is where I first met Anita Hill. In fact, the first time I talked with her, I recall, was at a luncheon at which Mr. Thomas was to be the featured speaker.

I learned at that time that she was from Oklahoma, and just out of the blue I said, "How would you like to come home and teach?" And she said, "I would like it."

And after the press conference that followed the luncheon, I told Chairman Thomas about my conversation and asked what he thought of it. He said, "Well, if that is what she would like to do, I would be all for it." And I said, "Well, do you think she would make a good teacher?" And I believe he said, "I think she would make a great teacher."

Following that, I arranged for her to be put in the process of filing applications which would go through our assistant dean. I wouldn't be involved in the paperwork until all of the recommendations were in. And sometime late in May I received her application, I believe, and all of the recommendations, and one from Chairman Thomas that was one of the most impressive, strongest statements in support of a candidate for our faculty that we had ever received.

Based upon that and, I believe, a conversation also with Chairman Thomas, I recommended to our provo [sic] that we engage her as a member of our faculty. That doesn't just happen perfunctorily at ORU, to get on the faculty because the dean says so. No one gets on the faculty at that school unless Oral Roberts approves, and after Oral Roberts, the chairman of the Board of Regents. And that happened in her case, and sometime in June she was offered a position on our faculty to take effect in August of 1983.

In 1984 I resigned as dean, to become effective in June, and during that time as she and I became better acquainted and I learned of her working on special projects, I spoke to her about my interest in civil rights, which had started with the act of 1964, and indicated I would be interested in some special assignments. And through her I was put in touch with Chairman Thomas, and led ultimately to my appointment in April of 1984, or maybe it was April of 1985, to a special assistant to Clarence Thomas at the EEOC.

During that time I had a number of assignments, one among which was, I wrote the 33-page report on the success story of Clarence Thomas, which was basically the improvements that he made and the progress he had made at EEO, and she conferred with me about that.

The CHAIRMAN. I'm sorry. I didn't hear you. You were assigned to do what?

Mr. KOTHE. I was assigned to work with the various persons in the EEO on the progress that was made from previous administrations. Anita had been working on a history of the EEO, and I put together a 33-page report which I labeled "The Success Story of Clarence Thomas," outlining the progress that had been made over previous years.

In 1986 ORU law school was closed, and Anita went to OU. I didn't keep in as close a [sic] touch with her at that time.

In April of 1987 a speech was made by Clarence Thomas in Tulsa before a personnel group, that I believe was arranged by Anita. She and I and my wife sat at the table together, and Clarence Thomas was there at that dinner.

After he spoke, he stayed at my home, which he has on several other occasions. The next morning we had breakfast together, and she attended the breakfast, and it was one of joviality and just one of joy. After that, as I recall it, she volunteered to take him to the airport in her sports car, of which she was quite proud.

During that period we were in touch only by telephone, and in April or May of 1987 she sent me a white paper on a project that had been under discussion for a seminar which she described as developing an EEO program that really works. The featured subject of that was to be sexual harassment, and I was to be, as she outlined in the program, to open the program on that subject.

We had talked about it, and all the time we ever talked about it, never once did she tell me or hint to me that she had had any personal experience of sexual harassment; never once in any of that time that that was under preparation, or in any other of the discussions we ever had when she was on our faculty, when she was in my home, whenever we were together at any time, that

Clarence Thomas was anything less than a genuinely fine person. In fact, she was very complimentary about him in every time we have ever talked together.

The last time she and I were together was in late 1987 or 1988, when we were both on the program for some personnel group in Tulsa. In discussing the preparation for that with her, I took what was generally my role of outlining the success story of Clarence Thomas. She took the technical part, and I think it had to do at that time with a case that involved pensions and civil rights.

And at that time, I believe Clarence Thomas had been married by that time, but in our discussions about him she was always very complimentary and I felt that she was fascinated by him. She spoke of him almost as a hero. She talked of him as a devoted father. She talked to me about his untiring energy. She never, ever, in all of our discourse, in all of those situations, ever said anything negative about him; and when we discussed the possibility of preparation for a seminar on sexual harassment, never said a word about her personal experience, or even her insights to any great degree.

In my experience with Clarence Thomas as a special assistant, I didn't have an office assigned, and frequently I would make my work station at the large conference table that he had in his office. Sitting there, I was able to observe him as he had discussions with some of the staff. Some of the employees would come, and other guests.

I traveled with this man for hours on end in automobiles, when we went through the swamps of Georgia together where he showed me where he was reared, and I have traveled with him by plane. I have been with him in business meetings, at banquets, at dinners in my home at least four times. We talked on to the end of the night in discussions of things that were of interest to both of us.

Never, ever in all of that time did I ever hear that man utter a profane word, never engage in any coarse conduct or loose talk.

Always it was sincere, many times religious. We were both reading together, you might say at the same time together, the books by Rabbi Kushner, the one, "Why Bad Things Happen To Good People," and I suppose that is almost prophetic, and the other, "Who Needs God?" In fact, as we last talked about the one, "Who Needs God?" he built a sermon on that that he later gave in the pulpit at the church where he was married.

The last time I was with Clarence Thomas, he was our speaker at the Oklahoma Bar Association prayer breakfast, and on that occasion he told the story of his life and his spiritual experience, at the close of which he gave a prayer that brought tears to my eyes and many others there. That day we heard a man of God talk.

I have been with this man. He is a man of strength. He is a man of character. He is a man of high moral standing, and I tell you that it is not possible that he could be linked with the kinds of things that have [sic] alleged against him here. If it were true, it is the greatest Jekyll and Hyde story in the history of mankind. This is a good man, a man I have known, and a man I respect, and a man I think is worthy of a position on the United States Supreme Court.

❏

TESTIMONY OF JOHN N. DOGGETT

Mr. DOGGETT. . . . It was difficult for me to make a decision to come here, but I felt I had no choice. When I left, graduated from Claremont Men's College, I went to Yale Law School, and in my third year at Yale Law School, Clarence Thomas came as a first year student. My class at Yale Law School was the largest number of black students ever to be admitted at Yale Law School, and half of those who came never graduated.

My first year at Yale Law School also was the time that there was the Black Panther trial, that the hippies and the yippies came to New Haven. It was a tumultuous time, and my experience at Yale Law School was a time where we said, as black students, "We are going to be the best possible people we can, and we are going to work on admission standards that guarantee that we get the best people we can possibly get." Clarence Thomas was one of those people.

In my senior year, in my third year at Yale Law School, one of the things we all did, we black law students, was to put together a seminar, a pre-entrance program, a week or so, in conjunction with the administration, to make sure that we could tell our colleagues about the ropes, so that they could maximize their performance. And I remember some of the students who had come before me saying, "It is impossible for black students to score the same on the law school admissions test as whites. It is impossible for black students to have the same GPAs."

And there were a handful of us who said that was—well, this is the Senate, and there are people who don't like obscenity—but there were a handful of people who had a very strong and negative reaction to that. And I remember with pride when the dean of Yale Law School was able to come up to some of those people and say, "I have in my hand a list of 15 applicants who are black, who have qualifications that meet the standards of anybody who is going to come to this law school."

. . . . I eventually went to Harvard Business School, where amazingly enough one of my friends was John Carr, the same John Carr who was here testifying on behalf of Anita Hill. And in fact, of Anita Hill, Clarence Thomas, and John Carr, John Carr is the person I am closest to because he is the person I knew the best. We were classmates at Harvard Business School.

I worked for Salomon Brothers during the summer. They offered me a full-time job. I turned them down. I joined McKenzie and Company here.

I met Anita Hill at a party in 1982, as far as I can remember, and I say as far as I can remember because, gentlemen, I had not thought about Anita Hill for eight or nine years, until I heard—

until I read in the New York Times last Monday that she had made these charges against Clarence Thomas.

I was introduced to Anita Hill by a man named Gil Hardy, a Yale Law School graduate who eventually was a partner in the law firm that Anita Hill worked for initially. It is unfortunate that Gil Hardy is not here, and the only reason he is not here is that he is dead. He died in a scuba-diving accident off the coast of Morocco.

Gil Hardy knew Clarence and knew Anita more than anybody I know, and if he was here, we probably would not be here now.

I talked to Clarence on a number of occasions, and one of the reasons I came forward is that I remember those conversations, and Clarence told me—and let me tell you, at this time I was a Democrat, at this time I really had some reservations about whether or not the Reagan revolution was good for this country, at this time I was being hammered by Reagonites [sic], because of my attitudes, and when I found out that somebody who had been a classmate of mine who I had assisted at Yale Law School was now in the position of being one of the top-breaking [sic] blacks in the Reagan administration, I wanted to go talk to this man and find out what was going on, because I knew he would tell me the truth.

One of the things that Clarence Thomas told me that really stuck in my mind, and one of the reason [sic] I said I've got to get this information to this committee and let them decide whether or not it is valuable, is that he said, "John, they call me an Uncle Tom. They are at my back. They are looking for anything they can use to take me out." He was quite aware of the scrutiny that he was under and the fact that his positions were very unpopular.

I also remember him talking about Bradford Reynolds, who at that time was the Assistant Attorney General for Civil Rights, and many of us, including myself, complained that this man was not qualified to lead the civil rights effort of the Justice Department. He said, "John, the Reagan administration went to every black Republican lawyer it knew, and they all turned the job down, and so nobody can complaint [sic] about Brad Reynolds being there. But I will tell you, one of my jobs is to make sure that I can try to keep this guy honest."

John Carr and I went to business school together. He was in the joint program. I had practiced seven years after Yale Law School and had decided that the only way to help poor people and people who were opposed [sic] was to learn more about how the economic system worked, to learn more about how businesses worked.

Since John was in the joint degree program, after I graduated from Harvard and came down to Washington, D.C., he remained at Harvard for another year and then went to New York.

In all the years that I have known John Carr, he has never mentioned knowing Anita Hill, and yet she stated that she dated that man and he said here that he would not call it dating.

In all the years that I have known Clarence Thomas, except for knowing that Anita Hill worked for him, he never mentioned her name. We never had any conversations about her. He mentioned the names of a number of friends. At times, it was clear he was very interested in trying to get me to know more black Republican conservatives, hoping to be able to convert me to the cause. He was not successful. But he never mentioned her.

And all the times that I had conversations with Anita Hill on the telephone and in person, that I observed her at parties of black Yale Law School graduates, she never ever talked about Clarence Thomas or talked about any problems or anything about that man.

I did have an experience with Ms. Hill just before she left to go to Oral Roberts University. And but for that experience, I would not be here, because other than that, my experience and relationships [sic] with Anita Hill was what I would consider very normal, cordial, and I thought of her as a decent person.

As you know, I submitted an affidavit to you. Ever since this committee released that affidavit to the press, the press has come to me saying would you talk about that affidavit. I said no, I am an attorney, I do not feel that is appropriate for me to discuss anything that is going to be discussed by this committee, before the committee has an opportunity to discuss it with me. . . . There are many things that I could say. There are many things that I will say. I stand behind the affidavit that I submitted to you, and I look forward to the time when this body and your colleagues vote on the nomination of Clarence Thomas, and I very much hope that you confirm Clarence Thomas. . . . But I will tell you, Senators, I am not here for any other reason than to say I had information that I thought would be of use to you. You have decided this information is useful, and when this process is over, except possibly talking to people as I leave this building, I hope to never have to talk about this again.

◻

TESTIMONY OF CARLTON STEWART

Mr. STEWART. Good evening, Senators, Senator Thurmond— I see that Senator Biden's seat is empty—and other distinguished members of the committee.

My name is Carleton [sic] Stewart. I am a graduate of Holy Cross College and the University of Georgia Law School. I was formerly house counsel to Shell Oil Company, in Houston, Texas, and Delta Airlines, in Atlanta, Georgia, respectively.

Additionally, I was a senior trial attorney with the Equal Employment Opportunity Commission, in Atlanta, Georgia, and later a special assistant to Judge Clarence Thomas, in Washington. Subsequently, I was as [sic] partner in the law firm of Arrington & Hallowell, in Atlanta, Georgia, and I am currently a principal in the Stewart firm in Atlanta, Georgia.

As aforestated [sic], I was a special assistant to Judge Clarence Thomas at the Equal Employment Opportunity Commission during much of the time that Anita Hill was employed there. At no time, did I hear any complaints from Ms. Hill concerning sexual harassment. At no time during my tenure at EEOC, did I observe or hear anything relative to sexual harassment by Judge Clarence Thomas.

In August of 1991, I ran into Ms. Anita Hill at the American Bar Association Convention, in Atlanta, Georgia, whereupon she stated, in the presence of Stanley Grayson, how great Clarence's nomination was and how much he deserved it. We went on to discuss Judge Clarence Thomas at [sic] our tenure at EEOC for an additional 30 or so minutes. There was no mention of sexual harassment nor anything negative about Judge Thomas stated during that time.

Senator THURMOND. Would you pull the microphone closer to you, so that people in the back can hear you?

Mr. STEWART. Okay. I will boom for you.

I have known Judge Clarence Thomas for more than 30 years, and I find the allegations by Ms. Hill not only ludicrous, but totally inconsistent and inapposite to his principles and his personality.

I will shorten this, so that we can get on with this. Thank you.

Senator DeCONCINI. Mr. Grayson?

❑

TESTIMONY OF STANLEY GRAYSON

Mr. GRAYSON. Thank you, Mr. Chairman, Senator Thurmond, members of this Judiciary Committee.

My name is Stanley E. Grayson. I reside in the city and State of New York. I am a vice president at the investment banking firm of Goldman Sachs & Company. Immediately prior to joining Goldman Sachs, approximately 20 months ago, I served as the Deputy Mayor for Finance and Economic Development for the City of New York.

I am a graduate of the University of Michigan Law School and the College of the Holy Cross.

During the weekend of August 10, 1991, while at the hotel and conference headquarters for the American Bar Association's convention, in Atlanta, Georgia, I was introduced to Professor Anita Hill by Mr. Carleton [sic] Stewart.

At this meeting, Ms. Hill, Mr. Stewart and I sat and conversed for at least 30 minutes. During the course of our conversation, in the presence of Mr. Stewart, Ms. Hill expressed her pleasure with Judge Thomas' nomination, and stated that he deserved it.

During this time, Ms. Hill made no mention of any sexual harassment by Judge Thomas, nor did she in any way indicate anything that might call into question the character or fitness of Judge Thomas for the U.S. Supreme Court. To the contrary, she seemed to take great pride in the fact that she had been a member of Judge Thomas' staff at the Equal Employment Opportunity Commission.

❑

W*itness John N. Doggett was asked to elaborate on the affidavit he previously had provided to the Committee.*

❏

Senator SPECTER. Mr. Doggett, turning to your affidavit, and I am going to ask you for the conclusions first before you comment on the substance of your statement. And permit me to comment, I found your testimony of your professional background extremely, enormously impressive.

And let me now move to the last line in the third full paragraph where you—well, why don't you read the last sentence in the third full paragraph on page 2, if you would, please?

Mr. DOGGETT. "I came away from her 'going away' party feeling that she was somewhat unstable and that in my case she had fantasized about my being interested in her romantically."

Senator SPECTER. And, if you would now, Mr. Doggett, read the paragraph on page 3?

Mr. DOGGETT. "It was my opinion at that time, and is my opinion now, that Ms. Hill's fantasies about my sexual interest in her were an indication of the fact that she was having a problem with being rejected by men she was attracted to. Her statements and actions in my presence during the time when she alleges that Clarence Thomas harassed her were totally inconsistent with her current descriptions and are, in my opinion, yet another example of her ability to fabricate the idea that someone was interested in her when in fact no such interest existed."

❏

Senator SPECTER. Now, Mr. Doggett, what happened between you and Professor Hill which led you to conclude that she was fantasizing?

Mr. DOGGETT. At a "going away" party for Anita Hill before she went to Oral Roberts University Law School, soon after I arrived and relatively early in that "going away" party she asked me if we could talk in private, and I agreed, having no reason to see that that was inappropriate.

And she talked to me like you would talk to a friend who you are going to give some advice to help them "clean up their act." She said, "Something I want to tell you"—and this is what I have quoted in my affidavit, and it is the only part of my affidavit that talks about her statements that is in quotes because it was emblazoned in my brain because it was such a bizarre statement for me.

She said, "I'm very disappointed in you. You really shouldn't lead women on, or lead on women, and then let them down."

I came to a woman's "going away" party who I really didn't know very well. She says, "Hey, let's talk in the corner," and she said, "You led me on. You've disappointed me." And it is like, What? Where is this coming from?

I don't know about you, gentlemen. Washington, D.C., is a very rough town if you are single and you are professional, for men and for women. Most people come here to be a part of the political process. They have legitimate, real ambitions. And it is a lonely town, a difficult town to get to know people because people are constantly coming in and coming out.

I came to Washington, D.C., to be part of the business process. I was not interested in politics. I wanted to be an international management consultant. And the first time I met Anita Hill I sensed that she was interested in getting to know me better and I was not interested in getting to know Anita Hill. And, based on my experience as a black male in this town, I did everything I could to try not to give her any indication that I was interested in her, and my affidavit talks about that in some detail.

Even when I was jogging by her house and she said, "Hi, John," and we had a conversation, and she raised the issue of, well, since we are neighbors why don't we have dinner, I tried to make it very clear that although I respected her as a person and as a fellow alumnus of Yale Law School, and as somebody I thought was very decent, the only relationship I was interested in was a professional relationship.

And, as I stated in my affidavit, she said, "Well, what would be a good time?" and I was in my jogging clothes and so obviously I don't have a calendar with me. I said, "Well, I will check my calendar and I will get back to you." And I checked my calendar and I said, "Looks like Tuesday will work. You get back to me if that will work and let's talk about a place."

Later on with that dinner agreement, arrangements fell through, she gave me a call and said, "What happened?" I said, "What do you mean what happened? I never heard from you." She said, "Well, I never heard from you." And apparently, we both had expected the other person to call to confirm.

At the end of that I never heard from you, I never heard from you, if I was interested in her the logical response would have been, "Well, since we didn't get together this time, let's do it again." There was no response, and there was a very awkward, pregnant pause and the conversation ended.

And I never saw Anita Hill again until that "going away" party where she dropped at [sic] bombshell on me.

❑

The proceedings were sidetracked temporarily when Senator Metzenbaum attempted to discredit Mr. Doggett as a witness by using against him unsworn allegations by a former co-worker.

The CHAIRMAN. Excuse me, let me interrupt for a minute.
Mr. DOGGETT. I'm pissed off, sir.
The CHAIRMAN. It is totally out of line with what the committee had agreed to—
Mr. DOGGETT. I'm sorry.

The CHAIRMAN [continuing]. For there to be entered into this record any unsworn statement by any witness who cannot be called before this committee, and I rule any such statement out of order.

Now, I apologize for being out of the room. Was there any—

Senator METZENBAUM. I was only reading from Mr. Doggett's own statement.

Mr. DOGGETT. My statement was not under oath, sir. That was a telephone conversation and they said we staffers would like to talk with you, we have a court reporter there. I'm a lawyer, sir, it was no deposition, it was not under oath, as Ms. Graham's comments were not under oath. And since you have brought this up, I demand the right to clear my name, sir.

Senator METZENBAUM. I was only reading from his statement, not from—

Mr. DOGGETT. I demand the right to clear my name, sir. I have been trashed for no reason by somebody who does not even have the basic facts right. This is what is going on with Clarence Thomas, and now I, another person coming up, has had a "witness" fabricated at the last moment to try to keep me from testifying.

Senator METZENBAUM. Well, Mr. Doggett—

Mr. DOGGETT. I am here, I don't care, she is wrong, and I would like to be able to clear my name, sir.

Senator METZENBAUM. Please do.

The CHAIRMAN. Sir, you will be permitted to say whatever you would like to with regard to, as you say, clearing your name. If there was no introduction of the transcript of Amy Louise Graham in the record, then that is a different story. I was under the impression that had been read from. That has not been read from.

Senator METZENBAUM. I did not read from that at all.

The CHAIRMAN. It has not been read from, and I don't know what else took place, but—

Senator METZENBAUM. I read from Mr. Doggett's questions asked of him—

The CHAIRMAN. Mr. Doggett, please, as much time as you want to make—

Senator METZENBAUM [continuing]. By the staff of Senator Biden, Senators Heflin, Thurmond, Leahy and SPECTER. My staff was not even present. I am just asking you if you would please go ahead and respond in any manner that you want to clear your name.

Mr. DOGGETT. Yes, sir.

Senator SPECTER. Mr. Chairman, you were not here, but what happened is that Senator Metzenbaum was reading to Mr. Doggett from Mr. Doggett's unsworn statement of the telephone interview—

Senator METZENBAUM. That's correct.

Senator SPECTER [continuing]. And that statement involved questions from Ms. Graham, who was questioned similarly in an unsworn statement over the telephone, and for Mr. Doggett to reply to what Senator Metzenbaum had asked him, since Senator Metzenbaum was basing his questions on what Ms. Graham had said, it is indispensable that Mr. Doggett be able to refer to what Ms. Graham said—

The CHAIRMAN. It is appropriate for Mr. Doggett to refer to whatever he wishes to refer to at this point, in light of where we are at the moment.

Mr. DOGGETT. Thank you, Mr. Chairman.

❑

The CHAIRMAN. Let the record show—and I would really like this to end—let the record show, and I am stating it, there is absolutely no evidence, none, no evidence in this record, no evidence before this committee that you did anything wrong with regard to anything, none. I say that as the chairman of this committee. I think your judgment about women is not so hot, whether or not people fantasize or don't. You and I disagree in that.

Mr. DOGGETT. Yes, sir.

The CHAIRMAN. But you did nothing. There is no evidence, the record should show, the press should show, there is absolutely no evidence that you did anything improper, period.

Mr. DOGGETT. Thank you, Senator.

Senator THURMOND. Mr. Chairman, would it be proper to expunge from the record, then, that information that came out?

The CHAIRMAN. Well, fine, but Senator, I would hope you would read from his statement of questions asked of him. I [sic] it is a little bit like if someone asked me over the telephone, "Are you still beating your wife?" and I answer yes or no, it doesn't matter. I am still in trouble. And then someone says, "I am reading only from your statement, Mr. Biden. You are the one that mentioned your wife." I never did.

And I know that is not what the Senator intended, but that is the effect. It is no different than just putting this unsubstantiated material in, and I want the record to show I don't think anything that is unsworn and I don't think anything in an FBI record is anything—up until the time it is sworn or the person is here to be cross-examined—is anything but garbage.

Mr. DOGGETT. Thank you, sir.

❑

When Clarence Thomas' nomination was debated on the Senate floor less than two days later, Senator Metzenbaum said:

"On a personal note, I want to say a word about the hearings. If a Senator is to fulfill his responsibility as a member of the

Judiciary Committee, he ought to be judicious. At one point in the hearings, I was not. While questioning Mr. Doggett, I unfairly asked him questions about allegations lodged against him. I should not have done that—it was not fair to him—and I apologized by personal letter to him that same day."

❑

T*estimony of a panel consisting of Patricia C. Johnson, Director of Labor Relations, Equal Employment Opportunity Commission; Linda M. Jackson, Social Science Research Analyst EEOC; Janet H. Brown, Former Press Secretary, Senator John Danforth; Lori Saxon, Former Assistant for Congressional Relations, Department of Education; Nancy Altman, formerly with Department of Education; Pamela Talkin, former Chief of Staff, EEOC; Anna Jenkins, former Secretary, EEOC; and Constance Newman, Director, Office of Personnel Management*

❑

TESTIMONY OF PATRICIA C. JOHNSON

Ms. JOHNSON. Good morning, Chairman Biden, Senator Thurmond and other members of this committee.

I am Patricia Cornwell Johnson, and I currently work as the Director of Labor Relations of the Equal Employment Opportunity Commission. I received my bachelor's degree from the American University here in Washington, and my law degree from the Georgetown University Law Center. I am a member of the bar of the District of Columbia, the U.S. Supreme Court, the U.S. Court of Appeals for the District of Columbia Circuit, as well as the majority of other U.S. Courts of Appeals.

I received my labor relations training at the National Labor Relations Boards [sic]. I moved from there to corporate America, then to a major transit authority, before going to the EEOC. I work in an area that is dominated by men and I have never met a man who treated me with more dignity and respect, who was more cordial and professional than was Judge Clarence Thomas.

Shortly after joining the Commission—and I must apologize

to my mother for making this statement on worldwide TV, and I am grateful that she is asleep—then Chairman Thomas became aware that I sued [sic] profanity in some exuberant exchanges with union officials. Chairman Thomas made it clear to me that that was unacceptable conduct which would not be tolerated. I was shocked because up until that time, such language had indeed been acceptable, almost expected—it made me "one of the boys." Chairman Thomas insisted that his managers conducts [sic] themselves in a manner that was above reproach and he held himself to that same high standard.

I had occasion to meet with Chairman Thomas alone to discuss labor relations and strategies. He was always professional. As a labor attorney with approximately 15 years of experience, I have drafted policy statements concerning sexual harassment, I have trained managers concerning what constitutes harassment, how to deal with such allegations.

Furthermore, with a previous employer, I was a victim of sexual harassment. It was the most degrading and humiliating experience of my professional career. I confided in friends and family concerning the best manner to confront it. I did confront it and I eventually left that position. But I must tell you that, during the time I had to continue to work with the perpetrator, I avoided contact, especially one-on-one contact with him, and since leaving that position I have never had any further contact with that man.

I do not believe these allegations that have been leveled against Judge Thomas. Moreover based on my professional experience, as well as my personal experience, I do not believe that a woman who has been victimized by the outrageously lewd, vile and vulgar behavior that has been described here would want to have, let alone maintain, any kind of relationship with a man that victimized her.

TESTIMONY OF LINDA M. JACKSON

Ms. JACKSON. Chairman Biden, Senator Thurmond and members of the committee: I would like to correct the record. I am employed as a Social Science Research Analyst at the EEOC.

When I first met Clarence Thomas in 1981, he was Assistant Secretary for Civil Rights in the Department of Education. My work required him [sic] to contact his office to secure certain data and information. After finding out the type of information I needed, Clarence Thomas indicated that any follow-up contact I had with his office should be through his aide, Anita Hill. He described her as someone who would help me navigate and put me in touch with the right people at OCR. He spoke in terms any mentor would use, explaining she was very bright and knowledgeable about the workings of OCR.

During that time, Anita and I began to have lunch and discuss both work and personal things. She referred to Clarence Thomas with admiration, and never once mentioned anything was going wrong at work. She seemed excited to be a special assistant to a very visible public official. I never saw any strained relations between them, whenever I saw them together in the work-place or at a meeting. She would generally look at him with a smile on her face and have the kind of positive demeanor that would suggest she respected and liked him as a person.

We often discussed the social scene in Washington. In the context of such discussions, it seems that she would have mentioned something, if she were having a problem at the office, even if she did not name a specific person. Subsequent discussions I had with Anita also yielded no mention of anything improper on the part of Clarence Thomas.

It is difficult for me to believe that Anita would follow her supervisor to another agency, if he was subjecting her to the things she has alleged.

I remember Anita Hill as an intelligent woman and one who would have found some way to retain her job at the department or find another in either the public or private sector, if she were unhappy.

After meeting Clarence Thomas through my job, I ran into him in the hallway of my apartment building and found we lived in the same place. We began to have numerous conversations about work, politics and personal issues. We became very good friends in the process.

I believe I know the basic nature of this man better than most people in this room. I believe, unequivocally, Clarence Thomas' denial of these allegations. This is a very honorable man who has the highest respect for women. He always treated me with utmost respect and was more sensitive to women than most men I know. He never engaged me in discussions of any kind that could be considered demeaning to women.

He was often troubled by those women he knew, both professionally and women, who were having difficulties with personal problems, particularly treatment by male friends, co-workers or spouses. He and I had numerous conversations about abuse of women, physically, emotionally and verbally. You see, Senators, he helped me pick up the pieces of my own crushed spirit, after I left an abusive marriage.

His sensitivity and honor, his respect for women, his helping attitude toward all people in need, makes [sic] these allegations even more ludicrous.

❑

TESTIMONY OF JANET H. BROWN

Ms. BROWN. My name is Janet Brown, Mr. Chairman. . . . I have known Clarence Thomas very well for 12 years. We worked for two years very closely here in the Senate on Senator Danforth's staff. He is a man of the highest principle, honesty, integrity and honor in all of his personal and professional actions.

A number of years ago, I was sexually harassed in the workplace. It was a demeaning, humiliating, sad and revolting experience. There was an intensive and lengthy internal investigation of his case, which is the route that I chose to pursue. Let me assure you that the last thing I would ever have done is follow the man who did this to a new job, call him on the phone or voluntarily share the same air space ever again.

Other than my immediate family, the one person who is [sic] the most outraged, compassionate, caring and sensitive to me was Clarence Thomas. He helped me work through the pain and talk through the options. No one who has been through it can talk about sexual harassment dispassionately. No one who takes it seriously would do it.

I don't subscribe to the belief that men, because they are men, don't understand sexual harassment. My husband, my father and my brother understand it. Clarence Thomas understands it. And because he understands it, he wouldn't do it.

❏

TESTIMONY OF LORI SAXON

Ms. SAXON. I worked at the Department of Education in the Office for Civil Rights from September 1981 until September 1982. I was 24 years old at the time. I was the confidential assistant to Clarence Thomas. In that capacity, I handled congressional relations and public affairs. My office was just down the hall from Anita Hill's during her tenure at the Department of Education.

I never saw any harassment go on in the office. The office was run very professionally. Clarence Thomas and Anita Hill were always very cordial and friendly in their relations. There was never any evidence of any harassment towards any of the female employees. I dealt with Anita Hill on a daily basis in performing my duties. She was happy in her position and she liked working for Clarence Thomas.

Anita Hill never indicated to me that he was harassing her. Clarence Thomas generally left the door of his office open, so if he had any meeting with Hill or any other employees, they were in view. He operated with an open-door policy with every member of the staff, regardless of gender. I never saw him meet in private with a female employee, without someone else present. Unless it was a group meeting and there were many staffers present, the door would be open and his secretary would be right outside the door.

Anita Hill was the only special assistant who accompanied Clarence Thomas to the Equal Employment Opportunity Commission, upon his appointment in August of 1982. Anita told me that she was very excited about the opportunity to work for the Chairman of the EEOC. She related to me that she was pleased that Clarence was taking her with him.

I believe Anita Hill's statements that she felt pressures to accompany Clarence Thomas to EEOC, because of fears of losing her job, are simply untrue. I and the rest of the senior staff of the Office for Civil Rights found other positions within a few months. That is how the process of being a political appointee worked.

I was Clarence Thomas' confidential assistant for a year. My job required that I meet with him at least once a day. He never made an inappropriate advance, uttered an off-color remarks [sic], or used coarse language in my presence. I was younger and more politically active than Anita Hill. I introduced him to my friends in Washington, the political community and very social settings. I was the first person to bring and introduce him to a luncheon with Thomas Sowell and others at the Capitol Hill Club. During this entire period, he never made any inappropriate actions toward me or any other female with whom I saw him.

I understand what women in this country go through in the area of sexual harassment. There is no place for sexual harassment in the workplace. I experienced perhaps a different kind of harassment, by being a victim of a violent crime. I know what it is to have one's face violated. I know what it feels like to feel helpless and humiliated.

Let me assure you in no uncertain terms that no harassment took place in the workplace at the Office for Civil Rights.

❏

TESTIMONY OF PATRICIA C. [sic] ALTMAN

Ms. ALTMAN. My name is Nancy ALTMAN. I consider myself a feminist. I am pro-choice. I care deeply about women's issues. In addition to working with Clarence Thomas at the Department of Education, I shared an office with him for two years in this building. Our desks were a few feet apart. Because we worked in such close quarters, I could hear virtually every conversation for two years that Clarence Thomas had. Not once in those two years did I ever hear Clarence Thomas make a sexist or offensive comment, not once.

I have myself been the victim of an improper, unwanted sexual advance by a supervisor. Gentlemen, when sexual harassment occurs, other women in the workplace know about it. The members of the committee seem to believe that when offensive behavior occurs in a private room, there can be no witnesses. This is wrong.

Sexual harassment occurs in an office in the middle of the workday. The victim is in a public place. The first person she sees immediately after the incident is usually the harasser's secretary. Co-workers, especially women, will notice an upset expression, a jittery manner, a teary or a distracted air, especially if the abusive behavior is occurring over and over and over again.

Further, the women I know who have been victimized always shared the experience with a female co-worker they could trust. They do this to validate their own experience, to obtain advice about options that they may pursue, to find out if others have been similarly abused, and to receive comfort. Friends outside the workplace make good comforters, but cannot meet the other needs.

It is not credible that Clarence Thomas could have engaged in the kinds of behavior that Anita Hill alleges, without any of the women who he worked closest with—dozens of us, we could spend days having women come up, his secretaries, his chief of staff, his other assistants, his colleagues—without any of us having sensed, seen or heard something.

❏

TESTIMONY OF ANNA JENKINS

Ms. JENKINS. Chairman Biden, Senator Thurmond and other members of the committee, my name is Anna Jenkins, and I reside in Silver Spring, Maryland. I am a staff assistant in the Office of Policy Development at the White House. I was not asked by the White House to give a statement. I went to them and asked if it was okay for me to give a statement.

I have been a Federal employee since December 1965 and worked for the Equal Employment Opportunity Commission from May 1970 to September 1989, with intermittent details to the White House under the Carter and Reagan administrations.

I was employed as a secretary in the EEOC's Office of the Chairman in the Executive Secretariat as a staff specialist. During my tenure with the Office of the Chairman, I served under five chairpersons, William Brown, John Powell, Lowell Perry, Eleanor Holmes Norton and Clarence Thomas. In September 1989, I left the EEOC to join the Bush administration, Office of Policy Development.

When President Reagan appointed Clarence Thomas as Chairman of the EEOC, I was the only employee left in the Chairman's Office from the previous administration. Upon Judge Thomas' arrival at the agency, I worked directly for him as his secretary until his confidential assistant Diane Holt and legal assistant Anita Hill came on-board. He brought them from the Department of Education.

Prior to Anita Hill joining the staff, she appeared quite anxious to work for the EEOC. In fact, she called Judge Thomas several times to inquire about the status of her appointment.

I recall the first day Ms. Hill reported to work at EEOC. She was very pleased and excited about being able to select an office with a big picture window overlooking the Watergate Hotel and the Potomac River.

I had daily contact with Anita Hill and Judge Thomas. We shared a suite of offices consisting of a reception area, conference room, kitchen, and five offices. Judge Thomas' conduct around me, Anita Hill, and other staffers was always proper and professional. I have never witnessed Judge

Thomas say anything or do anything that could be construed as sexual harassment. I have never witnessed him making sexual advances toward any female, nor have I witnessed him engaging in sexually oriented conversations with women.

I have witnessed Judge Thomas and Anita Hill interact in the office. At no time did the relationship appear strained nor Anita appear uncomfortable with the relationship.

I understand that at Anita's press conference she denied knowing Phyliss [sic] Berry. I was confused by her denial, since Phyliss [sic] Berry often visited the office while Anita worked there. I have seen them exchange greetings.

In closing, I wish to emphasize that I have the highest regard and respect for Judge Thomas. In light of my experience with him and the way I have seen him conduct himself around other females, I find this harassment allegation unbelievable.

❏

STATEMENT OF CONSTANCE BERRY NEWMAN

Mr. Chairman, Senator Thurmond and Members of the Committee: I appreciate the opportunity to appear before you in support of the confirmation of Judge Clarence Thomas as an Associate Justice of the United States Supreme Court.

I am both saddened and optimistic as a result of these proceedings. I am saddened because of the way in which the raw nerves of America have been touched. The raw nerves of which I speak are sexism, and racism, leading to mistrust between too many of us. Mr. Chairman, many of these feelings move just below the surface of this great nation. We are all victims . . . we are all hurt in some way by the side of America that allows bigotry and unfairness to exist. We must come to terms with what is unfair in this basically fair nation or we will be destroyed.

I am saddened for my friend, Judge Clarence Thomas and his family. All who are in public life must sympathize with their plight. All who choose public service as a profession understand that the public has a right to know whether we are competent. The public has a right to demand that we have integrity and that we do nothing to bring shame to the offices in which we serve. The public has a right to demand that we be fair to all . . . that we not engage in behavior such as sexual harassment or discrimination of any kind. In fact, the public has a right to expect that public servants will use all of their resources to insure that the diversity of the nation is represented at all levels in the public service and that the policies of the nation will result on all sharing in the nation's greatness. Those who choose public service expect that a certain amount of our privacy must be relinquished when we take the oath of office. But the public does not have the right to expect that we are stripped of all of our right to privacy. The public does not have the right to expect that public servants relinquish the guaranties that underlie the right to privacy such as those relating to freedom of speech and religion and protection against self-incrimination. The day that is expected of public servants is the day that the nation will not be able to attract the best to public service.

I am saddened for Professor Anita Hill. Her life will never be the same. I do not know her but I must believe that she must be a talented and conscientious woman or she would not have completed the tough educational requirements of a Yale Law School or be a tenured professor of a major law school. She must be a concerned black woman or she would not have chosen to work in Civil Rights at the Department of Education and the Equal Employment Opportunity Commission. What then was her motivation. Frankly, I do not know and will not even try to specu

I do believe that Professor Hill was caught in a whirlwind not of her making and was swept onto the public stage where the thirty and sixty second sound bites control. She was then in position where she had to move forward . . . she could not turn back the clock. How the power to turn back the clock would be helpful to us all on occasion.

I am saddened because I believe that the waters are muddier around the immoral and illegal practice of sexual harassment. Even in this day of enlightenment in employment practices, women in the workplace continue to suffer from practices of intimidation. Even today, there are male managers and executives in the workplace who believe that their only responsibility is to refrain from sexual harassment themselves. They do not accept the responsibility for insuring that all in their organizations understand that sexual harassment will not be tolerated. I am saddened because little of the discussion of sexual harassment that I have heard so far considers the rights of the accused. I know that is not the intent of the women's movement . . . of which I have been a part. The women's movement is seeking equality and fairness, but not by the imposition of an unfairness against the accused.

Mr. Chairman, I am also optimistic as a result of the proceedings. I believe that as a result of the hearings, Judge Thomas will be confirmed because others will know what I know—he has the competence, the integrity, the "true grit," and the sense of fairness that should be present in a Justice of the Supreme Court. I also believe that this process has made him an even better nominee for the Supreme Court than he was before this process. I know that he would probably not agree with me. But let me explain. This difficult process will insure that he will understand more than ever before the struggles that result in the cases that come before the Supreme Court. He will be prepared more than ever before to be sensitive to the types of conflict that bring cases before the Supreme Court. He will ask tough questions from the point of view of each side of every issue. He will not automatically accept the word of any party before the Supreme Court. That I believe.

I have known Clarence Thomas very well for more than ten years. He is my friend. That does not mean that we have not disagreed. That does not mean that we have not argued—we have. Through the years he has changed his views some and I have changed my views some. But I have not changed my views about the basic decency and integrity of this man. In the mid-eighties, I prepared a comprehensive report on the *Uniform Guidelines on Employee Selection Procedures* which required that I spend some of my time in the EEOC with some of the lawyers and other staff persons. Not once did I hear a hint of improper conduct on the part of Clarence Thomas. I would hear from time to time, that there was disagreement with his votes on some of the issues before the Commission. But that was to be expected.

Finally Mr. Chairman, I am optimistic that positive change will take place as a result of this proceeding because sexism and racism have been discussed in a very clear manner in the give and take between the members of the Committee and those who have testified before you. I believe that more Americans now more than ever before understand that the issue of sexual harassment in the workplace must be addressed. I believe that more Americans than ever before will understand that the issue of racism and stereotyping of one another must be stopped. And I believe that more Americans will in the end appreciate that this amazing governmental process does work—painful though it may be.

❑

TESTIMONY OF PAMELA TALKIN

As Chief of Staff of the Equal Employment Opportunity Commission from 1986–1989, I reported directly to then-Chairman Clarence Thomas. We worked very closely, traveled together frequently and spent innumerable hours together, both alone and in the company of employees. In all that time, Judge Thomas *never* acted with less than the utmost professionalism and courtesy toward me and other women.

It was Judge Thomas' unequivocal, and oft-repeated, policy that sexual harassment, even in its most subtle forms, would not be tolerated. And it was not. If Clarence Thomas was most intolerant of any behavior, it was the very behavior of which he is now being accused.

Without exaggeration, I would say we discussed the issue at least 100 times. Judge Thomas viewed such inappropriate behavior, even if it did not rise to the level of unlawful conduct, as (and I quote) "reprehensible", "despicable", "repugnant", and "disgusting". And these were the more charitable terms he used.

Judge Thomas was adamant in demanding that all female employees be treated with dignity and respect. He was always scrupulous in his approach to women and his behavior was absolutely above reproach. In the years I worked with and observed him, he invariably conducted all his interactions with women employees in a highly appropriate manner, with never even a hint of impropriety.

As someone who has endured varying degrees of offensive behavior from men in the workplace, I view myself as reasonably alert to such misconduct. It is in this context that I say that I have never known any other man who was as sensitive to and careful about the subtle issues and potential problems arising from relationships between men and women in the workplace.

This was a man who had a feminist's understanding of "sexual politics".

Judge Thomas was acutely aware that sexual harassment could occur even where a woman was not imposed upon physically or did not have her livelihood affected or threatened. Before it became the common view, Judge Thomas clearly understood and firmly believed that subjecting women to unwelcome attentions or inappropriate remarks also constituted sexual harassment. Early on, he foresaw and argued that conduct which creates a hostile working environment for women constituted a violation of Title VII of the Civil Rights Act. As we all know, that position was later adopted by the U.S. Supreme Court in the case of *Meritor Savings Bank v. Vinson.*

Judge Thomas was rigorous in ensuring high standards of conduct from all male employees of the Agency, particularly those men in supervisory and management positions. I witnessed his outrage and know that he took immediate action when inappropriate conduct occurred. He would not and did not condone even casual, inadvertent, or potential mistreatment of female employees.

Not only were male supervisors or managers forbidden to engage in any unlawful conduct, but Judge Thomas made it clear to them that the inherent imbalance of power between supervisors and employees required that persons in authority not act in *any* manner that could be even unintentionally coercive or make employees believe, even mistakenly, that their dignity was being compromised or that unfair advantage had been taken of them. To that end, Judge Thomas did not permit even consensual relationships between male supervisors and female subordinates.

Judge Thomas is a man of the highest integrity and character. In my 24 years of public service, over 18 of which have been spent enforcing laws against discrimination in employment, I have never encountered any other individual who was more committed to the establishment of a work environment free from all forms of discrimination and harassment.

❑

T he hearings ended at *2:03 A.M. on Oct. 14, 1991. The floor debate and Senate vote on the Thomas nomination were the next day. During the day-long debate, Senator Phil Gramm clearly outlined the politics that led to the second round of hearings.*

❏

How did the advise-and-consent clause in the Constitution turn into a political referendum about political philosophy?

We have elections to determine the political philosophy of the President. . . . In voting for President Bush, the people determined the philosophy of those who would be appointed to the Supreme Court.

Now what has happened, Mr. President, is that the people who lost that election are using the advise-and-consent clause to try to win what they could not win at the ballot box.

I ask my colleagues who are now searching for ways to repair the reputation of the Senate to realize that the reputation of the Senate has been diminished because, in reality, it deserves diminishing. I say to my colleagues, we ought to be debating about qualifications and about character.

Something is wrong when hundreds of people are sent out, including staff members of Senators and of the committee, not to get a balanced picture of the person, but for no reason except to find something to derail the confirmation—not because of the evidence that is found, but in an effort to deny the President of the United States the ability to appoint people who represent his philosophy, his values, and most importantly, the values of the American people.

❏

*S*enator Alan K. Simpson described how the confidential
information provided by Anita Hill became public.

❑

Let us remember how this thing got started. Ms. Anita Hill
did not want to provide her name and our chairman and ranking
member protected her. And then she finally came forward and
said let the committee see the information which she had. She
said it does not have anything to do with sexual harassment. It
has to do with his "behavior". She said please let the committee
see that, but do not let the public see it. And we did that. And
then somebody in this place, who surely will suffer some serious penalty, leaked that to the media. And then a member of
the media read it to her and said "What do you think of this, it is
all over town"—which it was not. And then that person said:
"You either let us go with it or we will have to go with it
anyway."

❑

*S*enator Hatch discussed how allegations such as Anita Hill's usually are treated by the Judiciary Committee, and how the committee treated this case.

❏

Mr. President, the way these processes work—and the process would work well if there was not so much influence from the outside—is that if an allegation comes in, the chairman then notifies the ranking member. In this case they both agreed to order an FBI check—it was an extensive check, the FBI did a good job—and then they brought it back and they felt they should notify the Members. Senator BIDEN notified everybody on his side. Nobody failed to have an understanding of what was going on. And he did what was right there.

These FBI reports contain raw data. You get everything from enemies to nuts, although in this particular matter it does not appear like that FBI report had any of those factors. . . .

If anybody on that committee before that committee vote had wanted an executive session, they would have gotten it. If anyone who wanted or desired to put this matter over for 1 week he had an absolute right to do it. If anyone had said in that open markup that, "I have read the FBI report" or "I have heard of the FBI report" or "I have been briefed on the FBI report," "and I am concerned about this allegation of sexual harassment; I think we need public hearings," I do not think there would have been any question they would have been listened to.

But there was a judgment made, as there is in many of these things, that a sexual harassment allegation 10 years old with all the difficulties that this case had and especially where the accuser had requested confidentiality.

The value judgment was made, and any Senator could have overturned that judgment. . . .

But someone on that committee breached the rules, waited until after that vote, and then leaked these matters to the press and did great harm to two, I think, basically good people.

❑

S enator Simpson provided a concise summary of Justice Thomas' testimony at the second round of hearings.

❏

I believe there was a very good thing that emerged from these hearings: Judge Thomas told the world with passion, anger, and accuracy about the cynical manipulation of the nomination process by the liberal special interest groups.

Judge Thomas told us how he was being lynched for being an uppity black man who dared to defy liberal ideology and think independently.

Judge Thomas gave a personally powerful and utterly convincing denial of any improper behavior on his part.

❏

P *erhaps the most impassioned floor speeches on behalf of Clarence Thomas on the day of the vote were made by his Senate sponsor Senator Jack Danforth.*

❑

Mr. President, let me start by thanking my colleagues on both sides of this debate for their tolerance during the past 3½ months. I know that I have been something of a pest hounding Republicans and Democrats alike, asking for support of Clarence Thomas, and fortunately for one and all that time is now drawing to a close until we get to the civil rights bill, of course.

Mr. President, when the President named Clarence Thomas to be his nominee for the Supreme Court, he described the nominee to be the best person in the United States for the job. Many people poked fun at that description, but this Senator believes that description was well founded.

I believe that Clarence Thomas is what America is all about. He captures in himself the American spirit, the tradition of being able to make the most of your life, and apply yourself and to contribute something with your life. I believed on July 1 that he was an outstanding choice, and I believe that even more today. During the past few weeks especially, Judge Thomas has demonstrated a strength of character which I think is extraordinary. He has endured, particularly over the last 10 days, the agonies of hell. I believe that as a result of that, Clarence Thomas is more sensitive to constitutional rights, to the necessity of legal protection of the people of this country, than most people who could conceivably be nominated for the U.S. Supreme Court.

In a way, Mr. President, this is a debate between those who know Clarence Thomas and those who do not.

What has been striking throughout the past 3½ months is the number of people who have known him very well, who are friends of Clarence Thomas, who have come forward.

Last week, a group of 18 women who had worked with him in various jobs here in Washington held a press conference and described, with tears streaming down their faces, the Clarence Thomas they knew and the concern they had with what was going on in the confirmation process.

I remember very well, Mr. President, the joy last July 1 when I was told by the White House of the Clarence Thomas nomination, and I remember talking to Judge Thomas on the night of July 1. I remember exactly where I was during that phone conversation. I was in the manager's office of the Shrine Club of Kirksville, MO, and I can remember the tremendous joy both in Clarence Thomas' voice and in my own as we visited over the telephone.

But, Mr. President, joy has long since left both Clarence Thomas and Jack Danforth and the many friends of Clarence Thomas. There is no joy in these proceedings and, no matter how the vote turns out, no joy is possible.

The joy that we experienced 3½ months ago has turned to pain, and the best that can be said is that in approximately another hour there will be a feeling of relief at the determination one way or another.

Clarence Thomas, especially in the last week, was liberated because he said to me that he does not need this job of being on the Supreme Court of the United States. He can survive without being an Associate Justice of the Supreme Court. Mr. President, very candidly, so can the country.

But what cannot survive, in the opinion of this Senator, is the values that we hold so dear as a country. I do not believe that our values as Americans can long survive the process that we have witnessed particularly during the last 10 days.

Mr. President, 10 days ago, this nomination had been won. The confirmation battle had been won. We believed that we had

60 to 65 votes in favor of Judge Thomas' confirmation. That was after the FBI report had been written. That was after the FBI report had been reviewed by members of the Judiciary Committee. That was after the members of the Judiciary Committee decided to a person that no further action was required, that no further study was necessary.

That was up to 10 days ago. And then, 10 days ago, the confidential document, and apparently details from the FBI report itself, were leaked to the press. And on Sunday, a week ago, this story went public. It was carried as the lead item on the network news and the headline item in the newspaper. That was the beginning of the process that culminated with the hearings before the Senate Judiciary Committee.

Mr. President, it is the position of this Senator that the process that we have just seen is clearly wrong. It is wrong for Clarence Thomas, and it is wrong for the United States. It must be stopped.

The business of interest groups fanning out through the country digging up dirt on a nominee, the business of leaks, of confidential documents, put out to members of the press, the idea that absolutely anything goes if necessary to stop a nominee from the Supreme Court of the United States, this whole process must be ended.

We in the Senate have the power to encourage the process, or we have the power to stop it. We have the power by the vote that we are about to cast to say to our country that the strategy of digging up dirt, the strategy of throwing dirt, the strategy of leaking confidential reports does not work.

Mr. President, I speak to those Senators who find the choice before us to be a difficult choice, who find it to be a close call whether to vote for or against the nomination of Clarence Thomas. . . .

The New York Times today took the position that in the case of a close call it should be resolved against the nominee. I believe that if that is the rule that we follow, that the burden of proof shifts to the nominee where charges are made, then the result of that will be to encourage just such a situation to be replicated again and again and again in the future.

The reason the burden against the accuser must be very heavy in a case such as this is to discourage exactly the kind of process that we have seen particularly during the last 10 days.

Mr. President, Clarence Thomas can survive without confirmation by the United States Senate. But if we vote against Clarence Thomas we reward a process which is clearly wrong. And for that reason, not for the sake of Clarence Thomas, not for the sake of the Supreme Court, but for the sake of the basic American standard of decency and fairness, I ask Senators to vote for the confirmation of Clarence Thomas.

❏

L ater, *Senator Danforth said:*

❏

. . . I would like to make four brief points.

First, I would like to express my appreciation to so many people who have done an extraordinary job on behalf of this nomination. . . .

My second point, Mr. President, is that this is not a vote on the issue of sexual harassment or what to do about sexual harassment; 100 Members of the Senate are concerned about it. . . .

But the way to fix the problem of sexual harassment is not to sacrifice up Clarence Thomas. The way to fix sexual harassment is to add remedies that do not now exist in the law for women who have been harassed and abused in the workplace. . . .

Third, Mr. President, no one, no human being ever should have to go through what Clarence Thomas has gone through for the last 100-plus days, and particularly for the last 10 days. It is not right. It is terribly, terribly wrong.

It is not true that the ends justify the means. It is not true that any strategy is permissible in order to win a political point. It is not true that in order to further a political agenda it is all right to destroy a human being. That is not what our country is all about.

We have developed a legal system in America to protect individuals. It is not worth any political objective to destroy an individual. That is what was attempted with respect to [sic] Thomas nomination.

Clarence Thomas will survive because he is an enormously strong person of very deep religious faith. But many people could not have endured this. Many people's lives literally would be in jeopardy if forced to endure the kind of thing that Clarence Thomas went through.

We must get our acts together. We, meaning the Senate and the various interest groups and the staff people here in the Senate, cannot permit ourselves to go through this again. It is wrong. And the one healthy thing that is happening is that the American people are speaking out and they are saying that it is wrong.

Fourth, and finally, Mr. President, the one really heartening thing, I think, from the standpoint of Clarence Thomas, is the number of people who have known him for a very long time who have felt so deeply about this nomination. This has been the case ever since last July. People who knew him in Missouri, who worked with him in the attorney general's office; people like his friend Larry Thompson from Atlanta, GA, who came up here and spent time helping Clarence and working with him because they had known each other working at Monsanto in St. Louis; people like Janet Brown, and Nancy Altman, and Alan Moore, and so many others who had worked with him in high office here in Washington; people at the EEOC, black, white, physically disabled, with tears in their eyes supporting Clarence Thomas. That is the heartening thing.

One thing that happens in the nomination process is that the enemies of a nominee tend to portray the nominee as some kind of a monster, and the great way to offset that is for people who know the nominee to come forward. And that is what has happened with respect to Clarence Thomas, and it is very gratifying.

Mr. President, Clarence Thomas is going to surprise many people on the U.S. Supreme Court. He is going to be a good, competent, decent, and fair Justice. He is going to be the people's Justice on the U.S. Supreme Court. In my opinion, it is a great moment for our country to confirm the nomination of Clarence Thomas.

❏

F *inally, the Senate voted.*

❑

The VICE PRESIDENT. The clerk will call the roll.
The assistant legislative clerk called the roll.
The result was announced—yeas 52, nays 48, as follows:

Rollcall vote No. 220 Ex.

YEAS—52

Bond	Danforth	Grassley	Mack	Seymour
Boren	DeConcini	Hatch	McCain	Shelby
Breaux	Dixon	Hatfield	McConnell	Simpson
Brown	Dole	Helms	Murkowski	Smith
Burns	Domenici	Hollings	Nickles	Specter
Chafee	Durenberger	Johnston	Nunn	Stevens
Coats	Exon	Kassebaum	Pressler	Symms
Cochran	Fowler	Kasten	Robb	Thurmond
Cohen	Gasn	Lott	Roth	Wallop
Craig	Gorton	Lugar	Rudman	Warner
D'Amato	Gramm			

NAYS—48

Adams	Byrd	Heflin	Lieberman	Riegle
Akaka	Conrad	Inouye	Metzenbaum	Rockefeller
Baucus	Cranston	Jeffords	Mikulski	Sanford
Bentsen	Daschle	Kennedy	Mitchell	Sarbanes
Biden	Dodd	Kerrey	Moynihan	Sasser
Bingaman	Ford	Kerry	Packwood	Simon
Bradley	Glenn	Kohl	Pell	Wellstone
Bryan	Gore	Lautenberg	Pryor	Wirth
Bumpers	Graham	Leahy	Reid	Wofford
Burdick	Harkin	Levin		

The VICE PRESIDENT. The nomination of Clarence Thomas, of Georgia, to be an Associate Justice of the U.S. Supreme Court is hereby confirmed.